STEEL FAITHFUL

Cover photos (clockwise from top left):
Pope Francis and Patti Gallagher Mansfield at the golden jubilee celebration of the Catholic charismatic renewal (see chapter 4); Wayne Alderson at the Labor-Management Prayer Breakfast podium (see chapter 6); J. T. Thomas of the Pittsburgh Steelers (see chapter 7); Sam Shoemaker (see chapter 2); downtown Pittsburgh today as seen from Mount Washington.

STEEL FAITHFUL

STORIES OF GOD AT WORK
IN PITTSBURGH

1952–2018

MICHAEL KING / BOB JAMISON / BRUCE BARRON

ADAM'S QUEST PUBLISHING

Steel Faithful: Stories of God at Work in Pittsburgh, 1952–2018

Copyright ©2018 Bob Jamison

Published by Adam's Quest
Pittsburgh, Pennsylvania

ISBN: 978-1-7329274-9-0 (paperback)
ISBN: 978-1-7329274-1-4 (e-book)

Scripture quotations are from the Holy Bible, New International Version®. NIV®. Copyright © 1973, 1978, 1984, 2011 by Biblica, Inc.™ All rights reserved worldwide. www.zondervan.com

Cover design: Studio Gearbox
Interior design and typesetting: Katherine Lloyd, The DESK

Photo Credits: Front cover (clockwise from top left): Tom Mangan; Value of the Person; J. T. Thomas; Pittsburgh Experiment; Pittsburgh view from Mt. Washington, Checubus/Shutterstock.com. **Chapter 1:** Detre Library and Archives, Heinz History Center. **Chapters 2 and 3:** Pittsburgh Experiment (all seven photos). **Chapter 4:** Tom Mangan; John Rossmiller; David Mangan; Tom Mangan. **Chapter 5:** Reid Carpenter (first and fourth photos); David Hillis (second and third photos). **Chapter 6:** Value of the Person (all five photos). **Chapter 7:** Hollis Haff (first, fourth, fifth, and sixth photos); Bill Stern (second and third photos). **Chapter 9:** Bethany Baptist Church archives; Charles Tame Jr.; family of Marion Adams; Richard Allen Farmer; Charles Hart. **Chapter 10:** Jay Passavant; Andrea Evans (both banquet photos); Bryan McCabe.

Contact the authors at Godatworkinpgh@gmail.com.

CONTENTS

Foreword	How This Book Came into Existence	1
One	Why These Stories Are Worth Telling … and Reading	3
Two	Sam Shoemaker: A Spiritual Giant Comes to Pittsburgh	9
Three	Shoemaker's Workplace Vision Fulfilled: The Pittsburgh Experiment.	37
Four	It All Started Here: The Birth of Catholic Charismatic Renewal	59
Five	The Master Connector and His Web of Influence: Reid Carpenter, the Pittsburgh Offensive, the Pittsburgh Leadership Foundation, et al.	79
Six	A Hole in His Head, God's Love for All in His Heart: Wayne Alderson and Value of the Person	105
Seven	Great Players, Great Messengers: The Spiritual Life and Influence of the Super Bowl–Era Pittsburgh Steelers	133
Eight	The Little Seminary That Could: Trinity School for Ministry	155
Nine	Not Your Typical Case of Racial Harmony: Bethany Baptist Church in Homewood	179
Ten	When One Door Closes, Another Opens: North Way Christian Community	195
Eleven	What Can We Learn?.	215
Note on Sources.	225

Foreword

HOW THIS BOOK CAME INTO EXISTENCE

I am a big fan of large breakfast events aimed at people who do not yet know Christ. I committed my own life to Christ at one such event in April 1986—the first "Gathering" outreach breakfast on the 17th floor of the William Penn Hotel in downtown Pittsburgh.

On that day, I heard Pat Williams, then general manager of the NBA Philadelphia 76ers, tell his story of redemption. I listened intently and checked the box on the card, indicating that I wanted to give my life to Jesus. I quickly lost some of my bad habits and embarked on an exciting process of transformation and of renewing my heart and mind that continues to this day.

During the decades since then, I have enjoyed fellowship, learning, and inspiration at many Christian breakfasts. But as the spring 2017 Greater Pittsburgh Community Leaders Prayer Breakfast approached, I had a bad attitude. Too busy to invite guests for our table, I had delegated that job to my lovely wife, and I knew few of her recruits. Learning that we would be driving to the breakfast with one of them, a local pastor whom I had never met, left me less than enthralled about the morning.

However, my tendency to be an ambassador for Pittsburgh kicked in once I discovered that our guest was a transplant from Florida who had been in Pittsburgh for only about 10 years. I started telling him about some of the great ministries that had originated in Pittsburgh: the Pittsburgh

Experiment, Coalition for Christian Outreach, and others. I found it curious that this pastor was unfamiliar with the depth of Christ-driven initiatives that had taken place in Pittsburgh over the previous 60 years. Sam Shoemaker's famous comment, delivered on Mount Washington, about wanting to make Pittsburgh "as famous for God as for steel" was foreign to him.

I wanted to tell this man as much as I could about Pittsburgh's great tradition of faith-based ministries, but my descriptions were often lacking in detail. I had heard for decades about Pittsburgh corporate leaders having Bible studies at the Duquesne Club. I knew of Reid Carpenter's work at the Pittsburgh Leadership Foundation and the many ministries that amazing organization had spun off. I was fascinated with the possibility that maybe God really did favor our Steelers because so many of them spoke openly of their relationship with God. Through my conversation with this pastor, I realized that many were unaware of how God had birthed incredibly fruitful ministries in Pittsburgh. I thought that these stories needed to be told.

When an idea weighs heavily on my mind, I take it to my friend and longtime Pittsburgh Christian leader Bob Jamison. In classic Pittsburgh style, this important meeting took place at Primanti's. After my third bite of the world's finest sandwich, I introduced the idea of capturing the great stories of Pittsburgh-based ministries in book form. We both recognized that many of the people through whom the Lord had worked to create such a harvest of ministry were getting old, and that some had already passed away. We had to act quickly or many of these stories would be lost forever.

Bob immediately loved the idea, and the concept came to life. He recruited his colleague Bruce Barron, an extensively published local author, to assist with research and writing. Eighteen months and nearly 100 interviews later, we had completed the text of this book. The stories told herein are as instructive, inspiring, and worthy of remembering as I had expected. I hope that you will be as inspired as I have been to follow in the footsteps of Pittsburgh's Christian heroes whose legacy is preserved here.

Michael King
December 2018

One

WHY THESE STORIES ARE WORTH TELLING ... AND READING

As rector of Calvary Episcopal Church in Pittsburgh's Shadyside neighborhood in the 1950s, Sam Shoemaker declared that his vision was to make Pittsburgh as famous for God as it was for steel. Shoemaker could not have foreseen that by the mid-1980s his vision would be relatively achievable, but for an unintended reason: due to the precipitous decline of the U.S. steel industry, Pittsburgh was no longer famous for steel. Steelmaking was visible in every direction from 1950s Pittsburgh, as far as the eye could see (which usually wasn't very far); it is virtually invisible in Pittsburgh today.

Were he with us today, Shoemaker would have to reconstruct his inspiring motto. Perhaps today he would aim at making Pittsburgh as famous for God as for Steelers. Nevertheless, the positive side of his vision—his desire to see God do mighty works through people in Pittsburgh—has also come to pass in unmistakable ways.

Over the last six decades, several Christian movements born in Pittsburgh have grown to national or even worldwide prominence. Through those grand endeavors and in many other less visible settings, God has worked through his people to produce lasting change and inspiration.

Pittsburgh as Sam Shoemaker would have viewed it from Mount Washington in the early 1950s. The Point, now Pittsburgh's signature park, was still a commercial area.

As the first-century Christian church was experiencing God's power in dramatic, life-changing fashion, one astute believer, known to us today as Dr. Luke, resolved to compile as reliable as possible a written record of those events, so that they would not be forgotten and could inspire generations to come. He produced the New Testament book of Acts, the only existing history of the Christian church's first years, which continues to inspire people nearly two thousand years later.

The great events that have happened in Pittsburgh, while not as momentous as the book of Acts, similarly deserve to be recorded and remembered. As Michael King notes in the foreword, the men and women behind many of these stories are aging or have passed away; their impact and inspiration should not go with them.

That is what this book is about.

One of the hardest parts of creating this book was deciding what stories to include. A few chapter topics were obvious, but beyond that set, a great number of candidates emerged. Knowing that no decision would please everyone, we resolved to be transparent about our selection criteria and to freely acknowledge that we have not exhausted the collection of tales worth telling.

Starting at the beginning of modern Pittsburgh, with the Christians who settled here in the eighteenth century, seemed too daunting a research task. As we sought to make the scope of work more manageable, Sam Shoemaker became clearly the most logical starting point. Not only was he a powerful, pivotal figure in the city, as a pastor of national prominence who chose to leave a thriving ministry in Manhattan and spend the last decade of his professional life in Pittsburgh, but he directly inspired much of what came after him. Shoemaker participated in founding the Pittsburgh Experiment and deeply influenced (though they had little direct personal contact) Reid Carpenter, who would become founder of the Pittsburgh Leadership Foundation. Two other chapters carry forward themes that were central to Shoemaker's ministry: his desire to foster joyful, exuberant, contagious faith (exemplified in the Catholic charismatic renewal) rather than staid churchianity, and his career-long drive to make faith relevant to the workplace (masterfully embodied by Wayne Alderson and Value of the Person).

We looked for stories that clearly illustrate the transforming impact of the Christian gospel on a large scale. We also sought to highlight enduring, quality efforts that have stood the test of time. While not ignoring the imperfections and missteps that are part of any realistic narrative of human endeavors, we focused on the positive impact of undertakings that a wide range of Christians would acknowledge as constructive and exemplary.

Those criteria introduced two biases: they tended to push us away from events too recent to have achieved recognizably enduring significance (every major story told in this book started in 1981 or earlier), and they favored wide-ranging collaborative efforts over the contributions of individual congregations. We are willing to accept the former bias, since newer stories can always be written in the future. The latter tendency, however, threatened to foster a false impression that the parachurch realm is where important things happen whereas the church is secondary. Accordingly, we decided to include two chapters on individual congregations. In doing so, we do not intend to suggest that these churches have been more obedient to God, more strategic in Pittsburgh, or more blessed than others. Rather, the church-level stories told here are compelling examples of God's powerful, providential work through particular congregations and reminders that no parachurch work can achieve sustainable positive impact without support from the church.

One other key criterion was that the stories had to offer interesting reading. The book of Acts shows very little interest in matters of church administration, except where controversies arose (e.g., the alleged neglect of Hellenistic Jewish widows in the Jerusalem church, the struggles over how to incorporate Gentiles into fellowship, and a managerial disagreement between Paul and Barnabas). Similarly, this book is not an administrative history or a manual on church leadership. We wanted to grab readers' attention and keep them reading.

On the other hand, we do depart from Dr. Luke's style in one important way. Acts records the history of the early church with virtually no commentary or evaluation. Christians have long debated, for example, whether the disciples were correct in immediately choosing a replacement for Judas or whether Paul should have continued on to Jerusalem despite a prophecy that he would be arrested; Luke refrains from giving his own opinion. In contrast, we presume to be mildly didactic at points, interpreting not just what happened but what spiritual lessons can be drawn from the great endeavors chronicled herein.

Finally among our criteria, we prioritized cases where we felt that our research and interviews could unearth valuable information not readily accessible. We are well aware that we have skipped over the two most famous ordained ministers in recent Pittsburgh's history, both of whom reached national audiences through decades of regularly scheduled appearances on secular television networks: evangelist Kathryn

Kuhlman, best known for her healing ministry, and children's television legend Fred Rogers. We do not mean to underestimate their importance, but we did not think that we could add anything new to what others have written about them.

We have no intention to claim a special place for Pittsburgh in God's heart or his strategy relative to other cities. We are telling Pittsburgh's stories because this is our city. Just as many of the initiatives described in this book have been successfully replicated elsewhere, we would be pleased if this book spawned similar publications on other cities.

Thanks to the revolutionary nature of electronic publishing, expanding this book would not be difficult. We encourage people who think we missed something important to send us their ideas, or even their own original chapters, at Godatworkinpgh@gmail.com to be considered for possible inclusion should we produce a second edition.

Midway through our preparation of this volume, we learned that Gary Scott Smith, a retired professor of history from Grove City College, was also writing a book on the history of Christianity in Pittsburgh. We contacted Gary, who graciously agreed to exchange drafts with us, at which point we discovered that there is surprisingly little overlap between the two books. Gary covers a wider range of topics based on far more extensive research, whereas we have chosen to highlight fewer topics in greater detail. Even in the two instances where the books appear to overlap most directly (both give substantial space to the Pittsburgh Steelers and North Way Christian Community), the content turns out to be more complementary than duplicative. In short, the two books are very different and we hope that you will read both of them.

We have had the honor of listening to and helping to preserve the stories of some truly incredible people (although they would humbly protest, in the spirit of Luke 17:10, that they were merely doing their duty) and the ways in which God used them. We hope that you will be touched by God as powerfully through reading this book as we have been in preparing it.

Two

SAM SHOEMAKER: A SPIRITUAL GIANT COMES TO PITTSBURGH

Among the historic names in Christian ministry in modern America, Billy Graham stands out as a master of evangelism. Tim Keller challenged intellectuals with his preaching and connected faith to the Manhattan workplace. Dennis Bennett, one of the first mainline pastors to be associated with the charismatic renewal, revived a dying urban Episcopal parish. Richard Halverson and Lloyd Ogilvie, both Senate chaplains, took the gospel to the elite and powerful; David Wilkerson boldly reached the down-and-out.

All these men of God are deservedly remembered. But if they are famous, then Sam Shoemaker should be even better known, because he was all these things rolled up into one person.

Shoemaker transformed Calvary Episcopal Church in lower Manhattan from a fading congregation into an exciting place for young people, applying methods well ahead of his time and holding open-air services in Madison Square. A compelling evangelist both one-to-one and in the pulpit, he was equally comfortable around wealthy businessmen and drunkards, founding Faith at Work (now Lumunos) and directly inspiring the birth of Alcoholics Anonymous.

Newsweek magazine called Shoemaker one of America's ten greatest preachers. Upon his death, Billy Graham said, "I doubt that any man in our generation has made a greater impact for God on the Christian world than did Sam Shoemaker."

In December 1951, Sam Shoemaker did something that no enormously successful New Yorker would be expected to do, unless he had been invited to become the CEO of U.S. Steel, Gulf Oil, or Westinghouse. He accepted a call to smoky, grimy Pittsburgh.

Sam Shoemaker

Despite the great impact and legacy of his work in New York, many accounts describe Shoemaker's decade in Pittsburgh as the most fruitful of his 40 years of ordained ministry. His influence continues to reverberate in Pittsburgh today; indeed, two of the subsequent chapters in this book derive substantially from his inspiration.

Nevertheless, and even though the Episcopal Church added him to its list of saints in 2009 (placing his feast day at January 31 on the liturgical calendar), Shoemaker personally is fading toward obscurity. Internet searches reveal relatively few references to him except in the Alcoholics Anonymous community, which still reveres him.

A book on God's memorable works in Pittsburgh has only one logical starting point: Sam Shoemaker.

FROM PRIVILEGE TO PERSONAL CALLING

Born in 1893, Sam Shoemaker grew up in a 28-room Victorian mansion ten miles north of Baltimore. He attended prep school in Rhode Island

and graduated from Princeton University in 1916. Raised in an Episcopal family, Shoemaker evidenced strong spiritual interest as a teenager, traveling to Northfield, Massachusetts in 1911 and 1912 to attend an annual summer conference aimed at motivating students for foreign missions. There he heard messages from such famed Christian leaders as John R. Mott (prominent in the Young Men's Christian Association back when it was intensely Christian in nature, and later a Nobel Peace Prize winner) and Sherwood Eddy, missionary to Asia.

As quoted in his wife Helen's biography of him, Shoemaker wrote in his diary that after his experience of Northfield, "The Christian faith could never again be the small, parochial, denominational affair that it once had been."

After Shoemaker graduated from Princeton, Eddy invited him on a mission trip to China. He arrived in October 1917, with the responsibilities of teaching insurance to Chinese students and meeting with small groups of inquirers into Christianity. He initially felt ineffective, but a visit from Frank Buchman, who had attracted large numbers of students to Bible studies as a YMCA leader at Penn State University, marked a spiritual turning point. As Shoemaker wrote 35 years later in *How To Become a Christian*:

> The test of a man's conversion is whether he has enough Christianity to get it over to other people. ... I could not do that. ... Individuals were seeking spiritual help, and I could not give it to them. Their faces still haunt me. I went out to China to teach in a school in old Peking. Again, men were seeking. I should have failed them in the same way, but out there I met a man [Buchman] who challenged me as to whether I had ever made a full commitment of my life to Jesus Christ. He held me to it till I did it. And the very next day a Chinese businessman made his decision with me.

Shoemaker remained in contact with Buchman and would later become a leading promoter of Buchman's Oxford Group movement, which involved intense sharing in small groups called "house parties" in which members confessed their sins to each other and spurred each other toward exhibiting the four "absolutes" of honesty, purity, unselfishness, and love.

During his remaining time in China, Shoemaker began to sense a calling to personal evangelism. He returned to the United States in 1919, doing some evangelistic work at Princeton and becoming ordained in the Episcopal denomination after just one year of seminary. He served a one-year assignment at Grace Episcopal Church in New York, writing his first book, *A Young Man's View of the Ministry*, during that time. In that book, he explained that he had entered the ministry "to keep people from missing the track in life, by showing them The Way."

In 1925, Shoemaker became rector of Calvary Episcopal Church, a declining congregation in an increasingly commercialized lower Manhattan. The church board was open to change and experimentation, and Shoemaker found the struggling parish attractive because it would give him "a chance to do something distinctive."

He did exactly that. Soon, ads on trolley cars were promoting Calvary Church as a place to find "personal religion, straight preaching, good music, a friendly atmosphere" and staff who "like to talk with people in search of vital religious experience." Shoemaker's messages highlighted people who had found God and learned how to share their faith with others. His private counseling sessions yielded many conversions, and church attendance quickly grew from 75 to several hundred.

In summer 1927, Shoemaker initiated outdoor evening services at nearby Madison Square Park. With a trumpeter playing hymns and members carrying signs that read "The Church has come to you. Will you come to the Church?" he led a four-block procession from Calvary to the park, where they sang and preached for all who would listen.

Driven by his deep concern for the needy, Shoemaker reopened in 1926 a Calvary building that had served as a local rescue mission in the late 1800s. The Calvary Mission housed and fed up to 57 men in need, most of them dealing with alcoholism. The rector was fully invested in this effort. His daughter Nickie Shoemaker Haggart recalled that by age four "I was just big enough to answer the front door to our apartment at Calvary House and let my Dad know that there was a 'drunker' there who wanted to talk to him. ... Dad never turned them away, and often he invited them in for supper. Other times, he asked them to go down the street to the Salvation Army to sleep it off, and he'd see them the next morning."

One of the many people to accept Christ at Calvary Mission, in December 1934, was Bill Wilson. Shoemaker and Wilson soon became friends; in fact, by January 1935 Shoemaker was deploying him to assist others struggling with alcohol addiction. Wilson attended Oxford Group house parties in New York as part of his efforts to stay sober. When tempted to drink while on a business trip to Akron, Ohio in May 1935, Wilson got on the phone in search of local Oxford Group members and connected with Bob Smith, a physician who had also sought Oxford Group support in trying to defeat his alcoholism. Wilson and Smith became the official cofounders of Alcoholics Anonymous, but Wilson pointed to Shoemaker as the primary source of the principles contained in AA's 12 steps.

Shoemaker's behind-the-scenes influence extended even further. According to his wife's biography, he initiated the idea of bringing a group of key Christian leaders together annually in Washington, DC to encourage and share experiences with each other. One of the participants was Abraham Vereide of International Christian Leadership, whose efforts to change leaders' hearts through prayer led to the establishment of the National Prayer Breakfast in 1953. A 2010 *New Yorker* article identified Shoemaker as the adviser who made "key connections for [Vereide] in New York and in Washington."

One participant in this fellowship group was Norman Vincent Peale, pastor of New York's Marble Collegiate Church, author of *The Power of Positive Thinking*, and perhaps America's most famous preacher at that time. Peale's daughter, Maggie Everett, recalled Shoemaker as providing invaluable encouragement to her father when he was criticized for "preaching to the balcony"—that is, being too concerned about attracting large crowds. Shoemaker retorted, "He's the only one who has people in the balcony!"

CALLED TO A SECOND CITY

Shoemaker celebrated 25 years at Calvary Church, New York in 1950. By this time he had not only a large congregation but a weekly radio ministry. That year he turned down an offer from a parish in San Francisco. In November 1951, Calvary Church in Pittsburgh, with support from a personal friend on the pulpit search committee and from the city's Episcopal bishop, contacted him. The presence of Ben Moreell, chairman of the Jones & Laughlin steel company and a former Navy admiral, on the search committee provided considerable weight to the inquiry.

Moreell and other members of the committee traveled to New York to meet with Shoemaker. Moreell later described his pitch as follows:

> We are having a renaissance in Pittsburgh, the renaissance consisting of the reconstruction of the physical parts of the city. ... But all these things are built out of perishable materials, and no part of that renaissance is dedicated to the building of souls. ... If we could show a Christian example for the rest of Pennsylvania and then perhaps for the rest of the country, and perhaps so have some influence on the rest of the world, it would be the most durable thing that we could do.

According to Helen Shoemaker's biography, she felt that the time was right for a move but he was reluctant, feeling that he still had plenty to do in New York. In an article called "How To Know the Will of God," written for *Faith at Work* magazine, Shoemaker recalled his initial skepticism:

> [The representatives from Pittsburgh] spoke of the great physical advances and improvements in Pittsburgh and said there needed to be a corresponding advance spiritually. This sounded exactly right, as the way to think about a new rector. But I felt as if they

were talking about someone else, not me. Not only did I feel they were looking for something too big for me to deliver, but it had at that time no "pull" for me. I felt like a hypocrite, taking their time and eating their lunch!

Yet he still considered the opportunity "magnificent" and he liked Pittsburgh's Episcopal bishop. As a result, he did not reject the offer immediately. As he contemplated it further, his wife pressed him to consider whether "it might be from God, and not just from Pittsburgh." After she left the house, Shoemaker wrote later, he had a dramatic vision:

> I said to the Lord, out loud so I wouldn't have any doubt about it, "Lord, do you want me to go to Pittsburgh? Because if you do, I'll go."
>
> Then something indicative happened. Sometimes he guides in words, sometimes in pictures. I saw a stone block come loose in a wall, with the cement broken and dry around it, and upend itself. So help me, it seemed to lean in the direction of western Pennsylvania. I went downstairs for breakfast and into the study, and tackled my mail. A little later I was musing to myself about something that was going to happen the next autumn. And something said to me, "There's not going to be any next autumn for you here."
>
> I never could get that stone to go back in place, nor escape the conviction that God was showing me his will. I never had three seconds of doubt that it was his will for me to go. And the wonderfully encouraging things that took place since have only deepened the sense that God was in that decision.

Shoemaker's strong sense of God's direction did not eliminate practical considerations as he negotiated the terms of his call. In a four-page letter dated December 14, 1951 to senior warden Lucius Robinson, he requested the following:

- an adequate pastoral staff, particularly to help with pastoral calls, since "I seem myself to draw such a heavy schedule of counseling";
- a full-time director of the Church School;
- hiring of his personal secretary, who was prepared to relocate with him;
- permission to continue his frequent ministry on university (especially Ivy League) campuses, which included two student conferences a year in New York;
- liberty to take up to three months of summer vacation, although "I have never taken more than two months."

The letter indicated that Shoemaker considered the proposed salary of $12,000 (equivalent to $114,000 in 2018 dollars) acceptable. The other details were also acceptably resolved and Shoemaker arrived as Calvary's rector in March 1952. A newspaper article shortly after his arrival showed his pleasure about the move: "I loved New York," he said, "but this is a much better place to live. … I never saw so many nice people gathered in one place as there are here."

REVITALIZING THE GOLF CLUB CROWD

According to an October 1953 feature article in *Fortune* magazine, Moreell's openness about his vibrant faith was not typical of Calvary's fashionable, staid parishioners. Social historians describe the early 1950s in America as a time of economic expansion, general satisfaction, and widespread but often superficial religious participation. Calvary as of 1952 may have had a tendency toward superficial spirituality, but Shoemaker did not delay in shaking things up.

One of his first initiatives was to gather younger married couples for discussions about the relevance of Christianity to modern life. According to one source, an opportunity to make inroads with religiously jaded people on the fringes of Calvary emerged when Shoemaker presided at a parishioner's funeral and mentioned to a young man who approached him after the service, "I haven't seen you around church." The man replied, "Frankly, the church doesn't have anything to offer me, and my friends think the same way." Shoemaker promptly embraced the challenge, inviting the man and his friends to meet with him and share their thoughts.

When the group convened at the Pittsburgh Golf Club, Shoemaker wisely started on his dialogue partners' turf, talking about something of keen importance to them: the free enterprise system. Over several hours, Shoemaker demonstrated that only God could serve as a suitable foundation for free enterprise. The group agreed to future meetings, at which he led the "golf club crowd" through discussions of the meaning of life, Christ's relevance to human need, the new birth in Christ, Christian fellowship, and how to live and witness as Christians.

Shoemaker had no hesitancy about calling these well-heeled, formerly nominal but unenthusiastic members of Calvary to radical conversion. When discussing the new birth, he declared without apology, "I am shocked to find how many people in our churches have never anywhere made a decisive Christian commitment. They oozed into church membership on a conventional kind of basis, but no one has ever effectively dealt with them spiritually, or helped them make a Christian decision." He even preached a sermon from Calvary's pulpit entitled "Are You Converted?" Using John 3:3 ("You must be born again") as his text, Shoemaker pointed out that the verse did *not* say, "Except a man grow and improve, he cannot see the kingdom of God."

In another portion of his 1952 message on the new birth, Shoemaker was even more candid about the dignified Episcopal Church's shyness concerning a call to commitment:

> Many people cover up their spiritual powerlessness, their unsurrendered, unconverted condition, by saying they love the quiet, steady nurture of the Episcopal Church; it isn't always taking them to a fire, or questioning whether they are converted or not. Yes, unhappily that is often true. And that is part of what keeps

the Episcopal Church, rich beyond almost all others in so many ways, from being the kind of spiritual force in the world that it ought to be.

It is truly amazing that Shoemaker could preach in such a way at Calvary and from other Episcopal pulpits and remain popular. But that was Shoemaker's consistent style, even in the hallowed halls of Episcopal seminaries. Canon Phil Ashey, an evangelical Anglican leader, recalled that his father was studying at the Episcopal seminary near Boston in 1950 when he met Shoemaker, who was known by then for "wandering the halls of many Episcopal seminaries to ask seminarians if they had a personal relationship with Jesus Christ as their Lord and Savior." When Ashey's father was unable to give a satisfactory answer to that question, Shoemaker directed him to attend Billy Graham's upcoming Boston crusade, where he firmly committed his life to Christ. Shoemaker's good humor, likable nature, obvious compassion, and solid intellectual pedigree probably gave him more freedom to inquire frankly about people's spiritual lives without causing offense.

By 1955, three years after his arrival in Pittsburgh, Shoemaker's achievements earned a feature story in *Time* magazine, which reported, "The casual young members of the 'Golf Club crowd' have found themselves talking religion at cocktail parties and even turning out for Bible-study meetings with 'Dr. Sam' at the H-Y-P (Harvard, Yale, Princeton) Club." In that article, Shoemaker articulated the vision statement that continues to resonate with Christians in Pittsburgh today (except for the comparison to the city's once-muscular steel industry):

> I like to envision Pittsburgh as a city under God, so that God would be the same to Pittsburgh as steel is to Pittsburgh. The backlog of Christian conviction and belief in this city means more to it than all the coal in the hills and all the steel in the mills. If these forces can be trained and mobilized, Pittsburgh might become a spiritual pilot plant for America.

FAITH AS AN EXPERIMENT

The 1953 *Fortune* article told the story of Putnam McDowell, a company executive who visited a Pittsburgh Golf Club meeting at some friends' invitation and was surprised to find young people who spoke openly of their faith and prayer life. As a result, McDowell said, he decided "to try this thing out" for himself. After finding that prayer led to improvement in his work situations, McDowell completed Calvary's confirmation class and became a Sunday-school teacher. He reported that Pittsburgh cocktail parties were spawning religious discussions, and that many participants' drinking habits had changed because "You can't go out and get plastered Saturday night and make any kind of an appearance at your Sunday-school class."

McDowell's testimony reflected the impact of Shoemaker's distinctive approach to Christian persuasion, reminiscent of nineteenth-century Christian existentialist philosopher Soren Kierkegaard. Shoemaker did present logical reasons for faith, but his main challenge was experiential: if you want to find out whether faith makes a difference, try it.

Shoemaker summed up his rationale for this method in the foreword to *How To Become a Christian*, which contained the messages that he used with the golf club crowd:

> Recently a young man of brilliant mind told me that for years he had tried to find God by reason alone. But he discovered there were reasons against believing, as well as reasons in favor of it. Then he found out that there was another way of approaching belief in God, and that was to put oneself in the way of finding Him through spiritual experiment. He had tried that experiment, and in rather a surprisingly short time he has become a profound and very persuasive believer.

Shoemaker's approach also resembled that of Alcoholics Anonymous, which in its foundational 12 steps calls on members to acknowledge the existence of a higher Power and to pursue "conscious contact with God as we understood him."

Shoemaker (at right) with members of his Calvary Church, Pittsburgh parish in the rectory.

In a Calvary sermon entitled "Act as If—Faith an Experiment," Shoemaker articulated more fully this way of introducing people to faith:

> In its earlier stages, the finding of faith may be very much like a scientific experiment. You take a hypothesis, you test it, you confirm or disprove it. Faith (real faith) does not move in an atmosphere of pious make-believe, but of open-eyed trial and testing. Science and religion can be quite close together in the all-important matter of the method of approach. As [poet James Russell] Lowell phrased it, "Science was faith once."
>
> Some will say, "But isn't it a kind of hypocrisy to 'act as if' when you really don't believe at all?" One could answer that it is not hypocrisy for a scientist to treat a hypothesis as true long

enough to prove to his own satisfaction that it is or is not. It might be hypocrisy if your mind was made up ahead of time, and if you were determined, no matter what happened, to hold on to your skepticism, or for that matter to hold on to your faith, no matter what "acting as if" might show. A real experiment, entered into with an honest and open mind, is an avenue of truth.

Mrs. Thomas A. Edison told me that her husband worked for eight years to create the common electric bulb. The world takes the incandescent bulb for granted. But it was one man's hypothetical faith that led to the discovery. Should we begrudge the few hours, or even months, or years, if it should take us that long to find God?

GETTING LAYPEOPLE GOING

Along with his challenge to try the experiment of faith, Shoemaker's work with the golf club crowd and in his parish exemplified two other themes that were never far from his mind: the crucial role of small groups as a channel for fellowship and spiritual growth, and the role of laypeople in the church.

In a report on his first five years at Calvary, Shoemaker described two types of small groups. The first type was for personal instruction, as represented by the "How To Become a Christian" course he had led seven times by 1957. Shoemaker indicated that nearly half of Calvary's church-school teachers had been members of his first such group in 1952.

The second type was the small groups that meet for Bible study, fellowship, and prayer, like those commonly found in churches today. Calvary had more than 20 such groups operating as of 1957. Many of them had grown out of the annual Schools of Prayer taught by Helen Shoemaker and promoted by the Pittsburgh Council of Churches.

In promoting small groups, as in many other instances, Shoemaker drew on Alcoholics Anonymous as a model:

> I have often said that the reason why A.A. moves in such tremendous power is that people with the problem of alcohol can see and meet and hear other people with the same problem talk

about it, and about deliverance from it, in a perfectly natural fashion. We need to see people who have been delivered from church-Pharisaism, and self-consciousness, and gossip, and leaky tongues, and small mindedness, and a host of other things that afflict us in the Church.

Shoemaker also viewed small groups as a place where laypeople could learn to talk naturally about their faith, thus becoming better equipped for lay evangelism. His favorite example of small-group evangelistic work was his disciple and friend Ralston Young (or "Red Cap 42"), a baggage carrier at New York's Grand Central Station whose infectious witness spawned lunchtime prayer meetings three days a week in an empty train car on Track 13. Young had learned about lay witness by attending "Faith at Work" prayer and sharing meetings during the 1940s in the parish house boiler room at Calvary Church, New York.

Perhaps the Scripture passage most frequently cited in Shoemaker's sermons was 1 Corinthians 12, which he used to argue that all believers, not just pastors, should be mobilized for active ministry. "The highly powerful and spiritual nature of these gifts," he said in one message, "shows us that in the early church were many people who did not just come to church, nor just support the institution, though they did this: they were channels of spiritual power. These were lay people."

Shoemaker practiced what he preached by taking Calvary laypeople with him on many of his speaking trips so that they could gain experience in expressing their faith.

These three principles—faith as an experiment, small groups, and lay mobilization—would become foundational to the Pittsburgh Experiment, born out of Shoemaker's work and designed to bring Christian faith authentically into the business world (see chapter 3).

SAM IN THE PULPIT

The best extant source that preserves what Shoemaker said during his years in Pittsburgh is his sermons. Beginning in 1956, Calvary Church printed his preached messages and made them available by mail for 15 cents each, or a reduced rate of $3 for the approximately 40 sermons that Shoemaker delivered in a full year. (The cost of first-class mail in 1956 was 3 cents.)

Shoemaker made *Newsweek*'s list of America's top 10 preachers in 1955, was heard each Sunday night on KDKA radio, and preached several sermon series that were broadcast on radio nationally. As a result, the demand for his printed messages was substantial. According to Calvary records, the mailing list was nearly 3,000 in May 1959, when the church shifted from an annual subscription fee to requesting donations. As of June 1960, 4,550 people were receiving the sermons by mail.

Calvary Church may not have fully recognized the future historical value of these messages, as most of the printed sermons are undated and the church's own collection depends on a few recipients who gave their copies back. Happily, about 250 sermons from 1956 to 1961 are preserved, carefully alphabetized in two boxes in the church archives along with a few audiotapes.

A review of the collection reveals Shoemaker as a humorous storyteller who frequently cited Scripture but preferred topical preaching over detailed exposition of biblical texts. He was well-read (citing numerous historians, political leaders, and philosophers like Blaise Pascal and Miguel de Unamuno); appreciative of the spiritual cycle of the liturgical year (an explanation of which formed one whole Sunday sermon); unabashed in speaking of the power of the Holy Spirit (even speaking favorably of the spiritual gifts of tongues and prophecy, though he is not known to have experienced those gifts himself); and singularly forceful about the urgency of personal commitment to Christ.

THE MEANING OF COMMUNISM

One aspect of Shoemaker's messages that clearly reflected the age in which he lived was the preoccupation with communism that pervades his books and sermons. Like many American political leaders of his day, he viewed the world as locked in a battle between freedom and communism and believed that the spread of Christianity depended on the victory of freedom. This perspective shaped his view of public policy and even of world mission. "All indifference to underprivileged people in this day," he warned in a 1956 sermon, "directly assists Communism, whether it concerns people in India or Africa, or whether it concerns minorities right here at home."

Shoemaker devoted a whole sermon in September 1959 to the implications of Nikita Khrushchev's upcoming visit to the United States, urging special prayers on the day when the Soviet premier would be in Pittsburgh. Even his choice of metaphors reflected his concerns about communism; when discussing the spiritual gifts of 1 Corinthians, he said that some (such as tongues) were distant from most modern Christians' experience but that others were "as contemporaneous as Castro."

But Shoemaker's reflections on communism always reinforced rather than interfering with his call to faith. In his view, the communist threat was forcing America to recognize its own weaknesses—poverty, materialism, lack of purpose—and should have been impelling Christians to greater intensity of commitment. "It is positively sinful to be as selfish about our religion as some of us are. Go and put spiritual bombs under people before the Communists drop hydrogen bombs on them," he stated. Though never puritanical in his moralism, Shoemaker found in communism's Third World advances a reason for Americans to devote their resources to a higher purpose than their personal pleasures:

> We are rich beyond any nation the world ever saw. But what do we spend our money for? Much of it is for our pleasure. We spend about eight billion a year on liquor and a like amount on tobacco. Yet [missionary and literacy advocate] Dr. Frank Laubach says two billion would be enough to train and send skilled men and women of the right spirit to help the world's helpless people to "come up" and find a better standard of living.

FAITH IN THE WORKPLACE

Shoemaker carried forward energetically in Pittsburgh the emphasis on taking faith into the workplace that he had pioneered in New York. In a sermon titled "A Message to American Business Men," he rejected the notion that business was for weekdays, religion was for Sunday only, and the two should not intersect:

> Let me say here that this kind of thinking is absolute heresy, from the Christian point of view. ... It puts religion way up into an ivory tower where it becomes irrelevant in the daily life of the world, and becomes rarer and rarer; and it puts business way down into the pig sty where money and sales are all that matter, and where it becomes rottener and rottener. This is as extreme a disservice to the religion as it is to the business.

He continued, "Business ought to be the main and chief extension of the church in the world. Your responsibility and opportunity as businessmen almost goes beyond mine as a minister, in the chance it gives you to help others to find God because they happen to work with you."

In his first year at Calvary, Shoemaker had a powerful impact on parishioners employed in the steel industry, especially David Griffith, a manager at U.S. Steel's Homestead Works. As the 1953 *Fortune* article reported, Griffith approached U.S. Steel's president during a strike and proposed letting the strikers vote by secret ballot to decide the matters in dispute. That request was not granted, but after the strike ended, Griffith launched weekly prayer meetings in his department, with both labor and management attending. The meetings were broadcast over a public-address system, making Homestead—site of the famous 1892 steel strike that erupted into fatal violence—a place of harmonious hymn singing 60 years later.

NO DUCKING CONTROVERSIAL TOPICS

Although Shoemaker was most preeminently a pastor and evangelist, social justice concerns did not escape his attention. In May 1959, he delivered a message entitled "The Holy Spirit and the Race Question," focusing primarily on the problem of racially based housing discrimination. He

A prayer group at U.S. Steel's Homestead Works. Leader David Griffith is at left.

urged support for Pittsburgh's 1958 fair housing ordinance, arguing that racial inclusiveness was an important feature of the early church, and described a Chicago neighborhood that had harmoniously become interracial without suffering a decline in housing values. "Thus," Shoemaker concluded, "there are no grounds for the fears that some entertain, unless they themselves become obstructionist and refuse to go along with these progressive steps that must be taken in the light of human facts, and certainly in the light of spiritual principles."

Shoemaker's boldness in discussing the gifts of the Holy Spirit from Calvary's pulpit is equally remarkable. In a two-part series preached in 1960, he spoke affirmingly of the gifts of healing and speaking in tongues. Undoubtedly aware that he was shocking some of his listeners, he acknowledged that "what I have been saying has probably gone right over the heads of some of us, as a fairly short time ago it might have gone right over mine. ... The things we have been considering certainly represent more of a stir, more of lay participation, more of active intervention by God's Holy Spirit, than is commonly found in conventional churches today. But the Holy Spirit is coming in new and fresh ways upon those churches." After quoting world Pentecostal leader David DuPlessis on the growing activity of the Holy Spirit within non-Pentecostal denominations, Shoemaker stated, "We close with only the question: Has He so moved within us?"

A FINAL MASTERPIECE ON SPIRITUAL RENEWAL

A journey through the spiritual depth and insights of Shoemaker's books and sermons can leave one wondering why he is not remembered like towering Christian philosophers C. S. Lewis or G. K. Chesterton, or at least like oft-quoted pastors such as A. W. Tozer or Charles Spurgeon. His messages, though sometimes linked to issues of his time, seem timeless and trenchant, full of contemporary relevance more than 50 years after they were delivered.

Perhaps this chapter will encourage a revival of interest in Shoemaker's works like Felix Mendelssohn's revival of Bach. If so, the place to start is his last major book, *With the Holy Spirit and with Fire* (1960). It contains some references to the author's own historical era, but much of it could be just as aptly spoken—and heeded—today.

Taking as his starting point the challenge of "communicating to a pagan, post-Christian world," Shoemaker wondered if the church had become too preoccupied with its own institutional life and "given too many hostages to contemporary culture, to say anything crisp and original." In an age of postwar prosperity, he warned that "prosperity breeds its own self-destroying properties, unless these are continually counteracted by some higher motivations and injections of spiritual responsibility."

Shoemaker described the churches of his era as making Jesus "an appendage to our Western culture" while all too seldom bringing their people to a living experience of Christ. He expressed particular impatience with those who rested smugly on ecclesiastical routine, intellectual theology, or doctrinal orthodoxy without spiritual power. Shoemaker quoted a comment allegedly made by a Lutheran bishop after a heavily theological session at the World Council of Churches: "The word became theology and did *not* dwell among us."

In contrast to this tame but often powerless form of religious practice, Shoemaker called for bold openness to the Holy Spirit's guidance. "I am convinced," he declared, "that most of us who call ourselves Christians are living far short of our possibilities because, though we give Him the lip service of belief, we do not know the stream of power which is the life of the Holy Spirit today." While granting that an emphasis on the Spirit could lead to excesses, he contended that the bigger problem in his day was neglect of the Spirit.

Shoemaker envisioned a "New Reformation" that would abolish the distinction between religion and life. Its "characteristic mark," he suggested, would be "Spirit-filled fellowships" of people openly sharing with each other their experiences of living by faith. (Consistent with this emphasis, Shoemaker devoted one chapter of the book to the formation and functioning of small groups.) Against objections regarding the difficulty of discerning God's will, he contended, "The difficult thing about guidance is not the receiving or recognizing of it: it is the truly wanting it, so that we come to God stripped, honest, without pretense."

Even in 1960, Shoemaker could perceive the growing disconnect between the institutional church and the surrounding culture. "I think the churches must all find some better way of exposing people to the Gospel than most of us now employ," he wrote. One might say that he was seeker-sensitive long before that term became popular. His answers to this problem, along with small groups, included having ministers "tell more stories about contemporary people" and incorporating greater lay participation, so as to bring people "into contact with current Christian experience."

Ever the passionate evangelist, Shoemaker discussed six essential qualities for effectively loving others into the kingdom of God: good manners, a clear grasp of human nature, humor, humility, honesty, and joy. Sensitive to objections that his emphasis on evangelism overlooked social concerns, he cited historical evidence that social impact follows spiritual transformation and argued that if Billy Graham talked more than he did about social issues, he would be putting the cart before the horse. His balanced statement on evangelism and social concern was unusually mature for his time:

> If some of the modern evangelists have been scant in their emphasis on social fruits, it may also be said that many of the social-gospel folk have been scant in providing a decisive and life-transforming personal experience of Christ. It is not a matter of "either … or": it is "both … and." But, as education is a matter of primary teaching and university teaching, they cannot both be given at the same time.

HE INTENDED TO PASTOR TILL AGE 72

Shoemaker seems to have loved every aspect of pastoral work, from preaching to personal counseling to administration, and he invested enormous effort in it. In one sermon he described his workday as normally 12 hours long, sometimes 14 or 15.

That devoted, single-minded lifestyle could not last forever. On April 3, 1961, at age 67, in a letter to the Calvary congregation, Shoemaker explained that his doctor had advised him against traveling to South Korea, where one of his daughters was living, and Japan. He continued, "When I further consulted him concerning when I should retire, and he found out that, after a bit of leisure, I hoped to do a good deal of writing and meeting engagements of various kinds, he suggested it might be well to take this action without too long a delay."

The advice must have been bitterly disappointing to Shoemaker, who had told the Calvary vestry in June 1960 that he intended to remain for five more years. But he heeded the doctor's recommendation, announcing in his letter that he was retiring from Calvary as of December 31, 1961. Reflecting his civic influence, the announcement made the local newspapers within two days.

On December 10, 1,500 people came to Pittsburgh's Carnegie Music

Hall for a "Salute to Dr. Sam." Those honoring him included numerous clergy, business leaders, Pittsburgh city solicitor David Craig, and Episcopal Diocese bishop Austin Pardue, who admitted, "Wherever I have preached around the world, people have come up and identified me because they read about me in one of Sam's books." Shoemaker urged the audience to work together in Christian unity to build a "spiritual renaissance" in Pittsburgh.

In his last sermon at Calvary, Shoemaker described a few of the upcoming radio, television, and speaking invitations on his schedule for 1962 and said that his upcoming year "does not look very much like a period of idyllic serenity. ... I am wondering when I may have to retire from my retirement! But I look forward to it all with enthusiasm."

Shoemaker retired to Burnside, his childhood home near Baltimore, although he made several return visits to Pittsburgh. Unfortunately, good

Shoemaker speaking at his retirement celebration,
Carnegie Music Hall, December 10, 1961.

health did not accompany Shoemaker into his post-parish career. In a letter to friends on July 1, 1963, he wrote that a brief respite from digestive problems had given him his "first real appetite for nearly two years."

Sam Shoemaker died on All Saints Day, October 31, 1963. In a memorial sermon ten days later, his successor in Pittsburgh, John Baiz, noted that several of Calvary's most outstanding younger members had told him, "Before Dr. Sam got hold of us, we were pure and simple pagans." Baiz summed up Shoemaker's unique place in American Christianity: "Not many Episcopal clergy had his unique emphasis and enthusiasm for the evangelical message of direct personal confrontation with the Lord Jesus. Someone once said to me that 'he was born with a Baptist heart into an Episcopal family'!"

The January-February 1964 issue of *Faith at Work* magazine contained a tribute to Shoemaker by Norman Vincent Peale, who wrote, "He was perhaps the most gifted genius in intimate person-to-person evangelism in our lifetime. … Sam used his extraordinary personal gifts to the maximum. God endowed him with a personality of unusual charm and he was equally at home among the highly placed and those of lower estate. … He was truly a universal man communicating a universal Gospel."

In addition to the Episcopal feast day now celebrated in Shoemaker's honor, Recovery Ministries of the Episcopal Church gives the Samuel Shoemaker award to honor leaders who promote spiritual healing in recovery from addiction.

GRACIOUS BUT INTENSE

Shoemaker was broad-minded as well as single-minded. He worked ecumenically with a citywide vision, calling for a Pittsburgh renaissance and ministering without regard to whether the recipients of his care belonged to his congregation. In fact, in a 1955 sermon in which he reflected on his first four years at Calvary, he emphasized, "I am continuously asking you *not* to disturb but to strengthen people's affiliations with other churches if they have them. I love to hear that what we are trying to do strengthens another church, Episcopal or otherwise." Despite his serious misgivings about some of the Catholic Church's theological pronouncements and what he considered its authoritarian tendencies, he affirmed that "we know some fine Christians who are Roman Catholics. We must look for every occasion of cooperation, for the expression of appreciation of them, for the exercise of Christian fellowship. Wherever we can find common cause and work together for it, we must do so."

That broadmindedness carried over to his perspective on giving. Shoemaker firmly advocated tithing but recommended giving only half the tithe to the church and the remainder to other charitable causes. This view was consistent with his unusually enthusiastic support of parachurch groups like the Fellowship of Christian Athletes and Young Life.

Sam certainly enjoyed life. Through his years in Pittsburgh, much of his socializing took place at the elite Harvard-Yale-Princeton Club downtown. (He never joined the Duquesne Club, saying that he could not justify both memberships, but in a 1957 letter he asked Calvary senior warden John Smith for help in accessing the massages available there.) But he was also intense, generous with his time, concerned for every individual, and diligent in devoting every part of his life to God, just as he called others to do.

On the first Shoemaker feast day (January 31, 2010), Calvary Episcopal Church held a forum featuring church members who had known Sam personally. At that forum, retired corporate lawyer Charlie Jarrett recalled the day 55 years earlier when, holding a law degree but unable to find work, he decided to ask Shoemaker to introduce him to someone of influence in the community who might hire him.

> I told him what I wanted. He said, "Charlie, I'm going to perform an introduction. Come on over in front of the fire and get on your knees." It was a rather unusual request, but when Sam requested, you answered. He knelt down with me and he prayed, not that I would get a job, but that I would open my heart and my mind to God, and that in his plan and wisdom what was right for me would happen.

That exchange, which Jarrett described as his introduction to a "life-changing experience" with God, was typical of Sam Shoemaker, a man never ashamed of the gospel.

A particularly impressive feature of Shoemaker's amazing ministry, and one in which he certainly resembled Jesus, was his ability to exude holiness and remain attractive to sinners at the same time. His sensitive, probing questions sparked curiosity rather than chasing people away. Nominal churchgoers from the golf club crowd and down-and-out drunkards alike were drawn to him, and he invariably found time for them. The church frequently falls prey to either legalism or indifference to the holiness of God; Shoemaker avoided both while unapologetically calling people into vibrant personal relationships with a living Savior.

Sam Shoemaker's life motto was to "stand by the door"—that is, to be at the intersection between the church and the world, connecting with people outside the church and calling them to Christian faith. We cannot sum up his life in any better way than how he summed it up, in his poem "I Stand by the Door."

> I stand by the door.
> I neither go too far in, nor stay too far out,
> The door is the most important door in the world—
> It is the door through which men walk when they find God.
> There's no use my going way inside, and staying there,
> When so many are still outside and they, as much as I,
> Crave to know where the door is.
> And all that so many ever find
> Is only the wall where a door ought to be.
> They creep along the wall like blind men,
> With outstretched, groping hands.
> Feeling for a door, knowing there must be a door,
> Yet they never find it ...
> So I stand by the door.

The most tremendous thing in the world
Is for men to find that door—the door to God.
The most important thing any man can do
Is to take hold of one of those blind, groping hands,
And put it on the latch—the latch that only clicks
And opens to the man's own touch.
Men die outside that door, as starving beggars die
On cold nights in cruel cities in the dead of winter—
Die for want of what is within their grasp.
They live, on the other side of it—live because they have not found it.
Nothing else matters compared to helping them find it,
And open it, and walk in, and find Him …
So I stand by the door.
Go in, great saints, go all the way in—
Go way down into the cavernous cellars,
And way up into the spacious attics—
It is a vast, roomy house, this house where God is.
Go into the deepest of hidden casements,
Of withdrawal, of silence, of sainthood.
Some must inhabit those inner rooms,
And know the depths and heights of God,
And call outside to the rest of us how wonderful it is.
Sometimes I take a deeper look in,
Sometimes venture in a little farther;
But my place seems closer to the opening …
So I stand by the door.

There is another reason why I stand there.
Some people get part way in and become afraid
Lest God and the zeal of His house devour them;
For God is so very great, and asks all of us.
And these people feel a cosmic claustrophobia,
And want to get out. "Let me out!" they cry.

And the people way inside only terrify them more.
Somebody must be by the door to tell them that they are spoiled
For the old life, they have seen too much:
Once taste God, and nothing but God will do any more.
Somebody must be watching for the frightened
Who seek to sneak out just where they came in,
To tell them how much better it is inside.

The people too far in do not see how near these are
To leaving—preoccupied with the wonder of it all.
Somebody must watch for those who have entered the door,
But would like to run away. So for them, too,
I stand by the door.
I admire the people who go way in.
But I wish they would not forget how it was
Before they got in. Then they would be able to help
The people who have not yet even found the door,
Or the people who want to run away again from God.
You can go in too deeply, and stay in too long,
And forget the people outside the door.
As for me, I shall take my old accustomed place,
Near enough to God to hear Him, and know He is there,
But not so far from men as not to hear them,
And remember they are there, too.
Where? Outside the door—
Thousands of them, millions of them.
But—more important for me—
One of them, two of them, ten of them,
Whose hands I am intended to put on the latch.
So I shall stand by the door and wait
For those who see it.
"I had rather be a door-keeper …"
So I stand by the door.

Three

SHOEMAKER'S WORKPLACE VISION FULFILLED:
THE PITTSBURGH EXPERIMENT

Don James was a wreck when he met Sam Shoemaker. Orphaned at age 17, he squeaked through high school and joined the Marine Corps, hoping to die in World War II. He survived, returned to Pittsburgh, got an accounting job, earned a college degree through night classes, and married. But he was still drunk much of the time.

With their marriage rapidly crumbling, James suggested to his wife that they attend church, but Joan would break into tears as she sat in the pew and contemplated the mess that the couple was in. Don kept visiting churches on his own. After several months he tried Calvary Episcopal Church, where he was struck by the congregation's unusual friendliness.

James returned for a second visit and met Sam Shoemaker afterwards. According to one version of their first interaction (probably embellished, but typical of both men in any case), James expressed his views on life and religion with ample use of coarse language, and Shoemaker replied, "You're the most honest man I've met in a long time. Can we have lunch together?"

After a few weeks Joan began coming to Calvary with Don, and a month later they told Shoemaker they were ready to join the church. To the Jameses' surprise, he asked them to wait six months, telling them, "I want to make sure that this is the last change you two ever make." Several months later, Shoemaker invited them to join a group of young married couples who would be studying his book *How To Become a Christian*. Through that series of meetings, James wrote afterwards, he "saw for the first time in my life the implications of professing a belief in Jesus Christ."

After that, James accepted an invitation to a businessmen's meeting downtown. He was expecting to encounter a group of "pious idiots," but instead he found men who were open and candid about their thoughts and prayer needs. "As I walked back to my office, I was a very confused young man," James recalled. "What I expected I hadn't found, and what I had found was better than anything I could have expected. Their honesty and sincerity were almost beyond belief."

Here's how James told the rest of the story a decade later, in 1963:

> I went to four [meetings] before somebody managed to dig out my problem. The Boss. Every time I looked at him my stomach would get tied in knots. Couldn't stand him.
>
> "Have you ever tried praying for him?" the leader asked. My answer you couldn't print in your newspaper. Anyway, he talked me into giving it a 30-day trial, which is what the whole program is based on—experiments in prayer, the kind where you talk out your problems with One who understands your kind of talk.
>
> To make a long story short, it worked. And in a surprising way. The boss called me to his office and asked, "What's the matter with you these last few days?" I told him I was praying for him. He laughed. We discussed my reasons for not liking him. We ended up friends.

James would eventually leave his career behind, graduate from an Episcopal seminary, and become the head of an organization designed to reach businessmen through small groups like the one that reached him.

James's experience illustrates three of Shoemaker's favorite strategies

THE PITTSBURGH EXPERIMENT

in action: mobilized laypeople, small-group interaction, and engaging in "the experiment of faith," which by this time was frequently presented in the form of a 30-day prayer experiment. Although this episode took place in 1953–1954, it is a quintessential example of what would happen hundreds of times under the auspices of the Pittsburgh Experiment—the lay-driven outreach program for businesspeople that Shoemaker and downtown church leaders formally launched in 1955, and which James would serve for nearly a decade as executive director.

EXPERIMENTING TO TRANSFORM SOULS

A pamphlet on the Pittsburgh Experiment's history, produced in the 1980s, traces the organization's birth back to Sam Shoemaker's meetings with the "golf club crowd" starting in 1952. In those meetings, Shoemaker

Don James, the Pittsburgh Experiment's colorful executive director for most of the 1960s, on Mount Washington.

frequently encouraged groups of businessmen to engage in 30-day prayer experiments. Ben Moreell, the steel company chairman who had helped to bring Shoemaker to Pittsburgh, was inspired by the change he saw in participants' lives: "They lost their diffidence, they were willing to talk about religion, … and there was a new life in their groups."

Moreell eventually suggested to Shoemaker that they should establish a formal organization to support and sustain this outburst of small-group enthusiasm. Moreell secured a three-year grant from a local foundation, and Shoemaker recruited William Cohea, a Presbyterian pastor and Princeton Seminary graduate, from Cedar Rapids, Iowa to become the Pittsburgh Experiment's first executive director.

The new organization's official launch occurred on February 25, 1955. An article on the event explained, "The Pittsburgh Experiment is designed to encourage people to bring Christianity into their normal daily dealings with each other. Primary emphasis is to be placed on the conduct of our business relationships." The original board contained members appointed by the pastors of five downtown churches, along with Shoemaker and Moreell. The Experiment's philosophy was summarized in three points:

1. It is a false view of religion to compartmentalize life.
2. The Experiment believes that business, industry, trade unions, [and] the work community as a whole is a character-building institution.
3. This is not new; the church has realized before that it does not exist for itself, but for those who do not belong to it.

Within the first year, Cohea supported and guided about a dozen evening or lunchtime groups, deployed laypeople to speak about their faith to other organizations, and planned the Experiment's first couples retreat, for 70 people at Bedford (in the mountains east of Pittsburgh) in fall 1955. The undertaking received national media attention including articles in *Time*, the *Christian Science Monitor*, and *Parade*. Cohea was even invited to speak at a World Council of Churches consultation on urban evangelism in May 1957, because the Experiment had gained such broad recognition as "a unique ecumenical evangelical approach."

Since small groups were the Experiment's primary tool, replicating them effectively in a welcoming, sensitive, non-preachy way became a leading priority. In a 1962 booklet, Don James (then the executive director) wrote that "Successful groups involve honest prayer, openness to drawing all present into the discussion without forcing anyone to speak, and time to share experiences and ask for prayer." Eventually—and perhaps predictably, given Shoemaker's frequent reference to Alcoholics Anonymous as a ministry model—the Experiment promulgated 12 crucial ingredients of small groups:

1. We accept each other as we are.
2. We share our struggles and successes, joys and pains.
3. We are honest. We set free the "real me" hidden behind the masks we accumulate.
4. We listen with every ounce of energy we have whenever someone else is speaking.
5. We never criticize or condemn when others share.
6. We never give advice.
7. We gather to care, not to cure. God does the curing.
8. We share in our own words. We share experiences from our own lives, not abstract ideas.
9. We trust one another completely. Everything we share is always confidential.
10. We are free to remain silent, if we wish.
11. We keep the discussion informal and natural, avoiding impersonal subjects.
12. We encourage one another to ministry beyond the group.

In retrospect, all the attention showered on the Experiment in its early years may have actually raised expectations too high. (In a 1961 letter,

James wrote that the publicity "backfired because we were not able to produce that which the publicity implied.") Organizationally, the Experiment in 1955 consisted of a large number of energized laypeople, one overworked young minister, and a part-time secretary. Cohea's report for 1956 highlighted an urgent need for a full-time secretary, but the Experiment's financial future beyond its initial three-year grant was uncertain. Perhaps partly for this reason, after three years Cohea left Pittsburgh to pastor a church in New Jersey.

The Experiment could have folded in 1958. Instead, trustee Paul Offill, a mechanical engineer whose search for spiritual meaning after his mother suffered a serious accident had led him to Shoemaker and then to the Experiment, stepped in as part-time director on top of his full-time job. According to the Experiment's history pamphlet, "God used this time of trial to reveal a hidden strength of the organization—the people themselves."

Although the program did not collapse, its uncertain finances made merger an attractive option. During 1958, the Experiment had extensive discussions with the Pittsburgh Council of Churches about coming under that organization's umbrella. In April, while Cohea was still in Pittsburgh, the Council of Churches considered creating a new Department of Laity within which the Experiment would function, but three member denominations objected.

The Experiment trustees must have anticipated a merger, because its archives contain a list of office furniture transferred to the Council of Churches on May 30, 1958. But the union never happened. It was scuttled primarily by the passionate opposition of Sam Shoemaker, an expert in distinguishing between church routines and vital Christianity. On September 9, he wrote to Experiment leaders in his distinctively candid, authoritative style:

> I know that at this time the future of a real effort to bring religion to the business life of Pittsburgh at the downtown level is at stake. ... I have had forty years of experience with the adjustment of a

fresh, vital spiritual movement to the life of the organized church. I think I have learned some things. It is in their light that I write you now what I think is a word of needed warning. ...

Enormous amounts of time have been consumed in committee discussions which might, I think, have better been spent in life-changing or building up strong groups. I cannot see any great enthusiasm on the part of the Council for this new association. So far as I know not one of their members has found time to go with one of us on a spiritual barn-storming expedition, and find out how we are in the habit of working. I hear, on good authority, that after the tone and subject of the forthcoming retreat was settled, some of the Council committee people who had had no contact with the Experiment nor our kind of retreats undertook to water down the subject of the retreat, until Paul Offill got it back again where it belonged. These may be straws in the wind, but they do not augur well. Most organizational religious leaders find it hard to understand what we are after. Are we not in grave danger of so hedging the movement about with legal and organizational restrictions that we shall find ourselves hamstrung and unable to act freely?

I was all for the initial effort to bring the Experiment under the Council as a Department of the Laity. I have watched the months-long negotiations with great interest and hope, and some misgiving. Now I am prepared to say that I think the proposed merger would be a fatal mistake. ... I think the time has come to break off the negotiations with all courtesy.

NEW MINISTRIES FLOURISH

Instead of folding or merging, the Experiment blossomed in the 1960s, responding to Shoemaker's challenge at his retirement celebration in December 1961, which became the organization's motto thenceforth: get changed (reorient your life around the Lordship and saving power of Jesus Christ), get together (meet with other believers to build intimate relationships and grow in the knowledge and experience of God), and get going (discern and respond to the physical and spiritual needs of those around you). Under James's tenure as executive director, which lasted from spring 1960 until his death of a heart attack on May 6, 1969, the organization grew in multiple ways even on its modest budget. (Total expenditures were still under $30,000 in 1964; James supplemented his income by filling vacant pulpits as minister-at-large for the Episcopal Diocese of Pittsburgh.)

The first clear sign of growth was that the conference program mushroomed. The Experiment's annual adult conferences at Oglebay Park in Wheeling, West Virginia were a hot item, featuring nationally prominent speakers; in 1962, for example, the presenters included Doug Coe of the National Prayer Breakfast, Bruce Larson of Faith at Work, and Sam Shoemaker. The 1964 Oglebay conference received 200 signups on the first day of registration and sold out within a week. Along with the esteemed speakers, participants heard gripping testimonies from Experimenters and—of course—had small group discussions.

Pittsburgh Experimenters packed the dining room at Oglebay Park in Wheeling, W.Va. for this 1968 retreat.

As the Experiment flourished and businessmen rebuilt their lives and their marriages around Jesus Christ, many of them found that the next priority need was their children. In response to popular demand, the Experiment began holding teenage conferences in 1963. Initially inexperienced at ministering to teenagers, James set up the conference schedule as he would for adults and quickly discovered that the teens were polite but restless; as a result, the program was totally reconceived in midstream, with a comedy night replacing the formal banquet.

Emotional testimonies remained at the core of ministry, however. Sue Zuk, Don James's daughter, recalled that on the way to one conference, her father shared the sordid details of his life story with her so that she wouldn't be shocked when he described them in his public testimony.

James achieved a better youth ministry solution in 1965 when Reid Carpenter, area director for Young Life, began leading the teenage retreats. In the same year, the Experiment introduced annual college conferences at Atwood Lake Park in eastern Ohio. At Carpenter's recommendation, British-born Christian rocker and evangelist John Guest was hired in 1968 to oversee the college outreach. (See chapter 5 for more on Carpenter and Guest.) In a 1967 Experiment newsletter, James wrote that "we could hold two of each conference per year, based on the number of applications we must turn down."

Second, consistent with Shoemaker's belief that social action should flow out of spiritually transformed lives, the Experiment took on new forms of service. The most substantial of these was Employment Anonymous, founded in 1962, which provided both spiritual and practical support to hundreds of job hunters. According to a 1968 booklet, the 15 volunteers at Employment Anonymous had helped 600 men find and keep jobs over the previous six years, while offering emotional support and encouraging them to adopt a habit of daily prayer.

In addition, the Experiment became a pipeline connecting its participants to ministry in Pittsburgh's state prison, with juvenile offenders, and at St. Joseph House of Hospitality, a Catholic residential program for the homeless. The director of St. Joseph told the *Pittsburgh Catholic* newspaper in 1966 that Employment Anonymous had enhanced Catholic participation in the Experiment. He added that the Catholics were easy to identify at Experiment meetings—they were the ones who didn't know how to pray spontaneously.

Experimenters also reached out sacrificially to assist youths in need of homes. Jim Leckie, who led a Christian ministry to at-risk youth, commented in 1966, "When I need help with temporary placing of children, trying to get 'fathers' for some of my boys, I know of no group who is more willing to help than the Pittsburgh Experiment."

Third, in 1960 the Experiment began a weekly talk show on KDKA radio, featuring Christians who were applying their faith to various aspects of their daily lives, which continued for over 20 years.

Fourth, the first round of replication began in this decade. In 1961

Pittsburgh Experiment executive director Don James (right) and David Craig, city solicitor and later public safety director, prepare for an Experiment radio broadcast.

Edward Meeman, a newspaper editor in Memphis, Tennessee who knew Shoemaker personally, wrote a commentary about the Pittsburgh Experiment, echoing Moreell's message of 10 years earlier: "Pittsburgh is famed for its physical Renaissance ... but is not this parallel rebirth of the Spirit even more important?" A photo engraver working at a Knoxville, Tennessee newspaper plagued by labor problems saw the editorial and suggested doing the same thing in his city. The Knoxville Experiment started in 1962 and had 200 participants when James spoke at one of its events in January 1963.

THE LONGEST-TERM STAFFER

Of the Experiment's many 1960s expansions, the one that had the most enduring impact was its 1967 addition of an associate director whose personal experience of Sam Shoemaker dated back to New York.

Paul Everett was a rising star in the executive training program at Macy's department store in New York when he interviewed with Ellie Hummer, head of the wildly profitable junior dress division. Everett, who had no church involvement, was quite unsettled when Hummer began the interview by saying, "I believe that God has a plan for me and I am trying to follow it in my business and personal life."

Despite his skepticism, he accepted Hummer's invitation to her young adult group, on Sunday nights at Norman Vincent Peale's Marble Collegiate Church. "The church at Macy's brought me to a church building in New York," Everett said later. Not only did he come to Christ and begin his spiritual growth at Marble, but he eventually married Peale's daughter, Maggie.

Shoemaker and James occasionally traveled to New York to speak at Marble's young adult group. After one of Shoemaker's messages, a friend of Everett's introduced the two, gushing profusely about how much Everett had already achieved. Nonplussed, Shoemaker shot back, "Paul, I really don't give a damn who you are, but what will forever excite me is how far you've come in your life. And I'd love to hear that."

After playing a leadership role among Marble's young adults, Everett, to his family's great dismay, gave up his business career to attend Princeton Seminary and then became minister of evangelism at Wayne Presbyterian Church near Philadelphia. Four years later, he was ready to look for a senior pastor position when Don James contacted him. Since Pittsburgh had so many Presbyterians, James wanted to hire a Presbyterian associate director, and one of his acquaintances at Marble had recommended Everett.

As Maggie Everett explained, Paul had just resolved in prayer that he would investigate any opportunity that came his way; otherwise he would have declined James's invitation. He had seen Pittsburgh only once, through a train window on his way home from serving in the Korean War. He remembered looking out at the smoky city on a dreary morning and saying to himself, "Thank God I'll never have to live here."

Paul and Maggie spent two days in Pittsburgh. He didn't think the job was right for him—until he saw Employment Anonymous. The Christian outreach to people facing the emotional strains of unemployment won him over. Unfortunately, Maggie still had no interest in coming to Pittsburgh. Paul phoned Don James and said, "I think I am called to this job, but we will have to wait until Maggie comes around."

Since the late Sam Shoemaker was no longer available, God picked the next best way to intervene: Mrs. Shoemaker. As Maggie explained: "We were invited to a fundraising dinner at a seminary and sat next to Helen. She was a very powerful person in her own right. She said, 'When I met Sam, my plan for my life was to be a missionary. But you couldn't go off and be a missionary with a husband who wasn't one. So I had to make a choice whether to be a missionary or marry Sam, and I loved him and felt I should marry him though I felt bad about giving up my vision. I look back on my life and think of all the things I would have missed had I not married him.' I don't know what it was about that conversation, but in the car after dinner, I said to Paul, 'All right, I don't like it, but I feel that's where we are supposed to go.'"

Paul Everett thought he might stay for five years and then take a pastorate. Instead, he spent the rest of his professional career at the Pittsburgh Experiment, retiring in 1995. When the Everetts moved to Connecticut to be closer to Maggie's aging mother, Maggie was the one who couldn't bear to leave.

Paul proved to be a great fit for a ministry that sought to love people into the kingdom of God. He exuded a vibrant faith in a calm, theologically broad way. He was fully committed to Shoemaker's style of bringing faith into people's daily lives, without the churchy language that erected barriers between religion and business. "Evangelical language is fine among evangelicals," Maggie Everett pointed out, "but not when you are trying to stand by the door and bring people in."

Everett also continued what had been a big part of James's job, serving as pastoral counselor to people whose needs were too complex or vexing for their small group to handle. James had been so devoted to counseling that Sue Zuk recalled many counselees—typically the unemployed or people coming out of prison—staying overnight in their home. Everett, more contemplative in nature, maintained long-term personal relationships and also introduced silent retreats into Experiment spirituality.

Joe Hines, whose association with the Experiment has spanned 50 years, was a beneficiary of Everett's long-term investment. In 1964, Hines became the first African American in Mellon Bank's management training program; four years later, a Mellon colleague invited him to an Experiment lunch group. Hines credits the Experiment with guiding his spiritual life from a "convenient activity" to serious commitment. He became part of a group of about a dozen Experimenters who led chapel services at Western Penitentiary, befriended inmates, and helped them through their transition upon release. Hines remained in touch with Everett even after Mellon Bank transferred him from downtown to an outlying location, and Everett supported him through a prayer experiment in 1989—more than 20 years after their first meeting—that led Hines to make a major career change and spend the last 15 years of his professional life as a high-school math teacher.

The Pittsburgh Experiment was replicated in many more locations after Knoxville, such as Jacksonville, Cincinnati, and Jackson, Mississippi during the 1970s. Its biggest push came from Norman Vincent Peale, whose

Foundation for Christian Living launched a "Guideposts National Experiment" in the early 1980s. (*Guideposts* was the name of Peale's monthly magazine.) Peale published and wrote a foreword for Everett's booklet *The Power of 30 Days*; his organization supported Everett's travels to launch Experiment organizations in additional cities and promoted the idea through occasional newsletters for 10 years. The first Guideposts National Experiment newsletter, in January 1982, reported on the formation of new groups in 42 communities across the United States and Canada.

Everett guided one other important change: the integration of working women. Experiment newsletters from the early 1980s chronicle, with trademark candidness, the need for sensitivity to men who felt threatened by women's entry into previously male-dominated professional sectors. The organization operated a pilot co-ed group for two years before making mixed-gender groups a core aspect of its ministry.

CLASSIC RECOLLECTIONS

The Pittsburgh Experiment has touched thousands of people, but its most inspiring legacy is in individual stories of people whom this ministry guided from worldly immersion and emptiness to spiritual transformation and fulfillment. Some of the stories are quite amazing. They might make you believe in divine "coincidence" if you don't already.

In 1978, Kerry Fraas was a young lawyer with two years of Christian experience but no firm connections with believers in his professional life. A client invited him to a lunchtime meeting where "we talk about our lives and pray for one another." Fraas was impressed by the level of openness and trust. "People could be their real selves there, knowing that it wouldn't be shared anywhere else," he observed. "I also liked that you could share or not share, and that people weren't trying to give advice or fix other people.

"I had lunch with Paul Everett, who made a point of meeting with new attenders, and he explained the Experiment to me. Although I also had a church, this became a spiritual home for me for 25 years.

"Many times, a new person would come and sit in stunned silence as to how real these businessmen in coats and ties would be in our conversations, because they had never experienced it before. It was quite moving when a new person would feel comfortable enough to open up, be vulnerable, and realize that people cared about them as we brought supernatural help to bear on personal issues.

"This lunch group became the most profound and memorable spiritual experience of my life. It helped me through my career successes and failures, financial struggles, and difficult relationships with bosses and coworkers, all with a clear head. And the retreats were fantastic. I had never been on a retreat where people could share so openly. There was so much laughter among the men that sometimes my stomach would hurt. (When I joined the board, I learned that on the women's retreats some people cried for three days straight.)

"I was involved in a mixed group for a while, but it didn't work for me. It was harder to be open and vulnerable, especially on sexual matters, with women present. I always felt that single-gender groups provided greater depth and authenticity.

"Paul was a great leader and a special human being—very charismatic but in a low-key way, open and vulnerable, sympathetic, a man of prayer and spiritual depth. The groups were largely autonomous and could have functioned without the Experiment's imprimatur, but it was good to have a leader available if issues arose. Also, the major events showed that we were part of a larger movement and making significant contributions to the region and the marketplace.

"My own father-in-law, a business executive, was facing marital struggles. A general marriage counselor wouldn't have worked—he needed someone who could talk with him on his level. He and his wife credited Paul with saving their marriage. And my father-in-law wasn't even involved in the Experiment. The executive director was more a pastor to the marketplace than an administrative leader."

Fraas was directly involved in one of the most memorable stories of the Experiment's history, recounted in the spring 1991 Guideposts National

Experiment magazine. Randy Purcell, a renowned jazz trombonist who had toured with the Maynard Ferguson Orchestra before becoming a stockbroker, showed up at Fraas's lunch group. After attending several meetings, Purcell shared that a client had accused him of wrongdoing and the company appeared to be taking the client's side.

"Someone from upper management was coming in from Philadelphia to decide his fate," Fraas recalled, "and we were praying for the meeting. I went to a Bible study at my home church that morning, and the pastor asked if I could give a ride downtown to a friend of his, a guest from Philadelphia.

"As we drove into town together, I discovered that he was the president of a stock firm. He said that he had a very sad duty to do that day. When I mentioned the name Randy Purcell, he almost fell out of the car. I was driving Randy's executioner to the meeting! I told the company president about Randy's search for faith and that we were praying for him.

"That afternoon Randy called me and said that he couldn't believe it but they had completely changed their attitude toward him, saying that they would support him in this issue with the customer and that he would not be fired. Randy subsequently became a follower of Jesus. He realized not just that God exists, but that God loves us and is willing to intervene in our deepest needs."

Jay Roy had an experience of failure at age 25 that left him aware of his own inadequacies. Up to that point, he had been a good, upstanding churchgoer; now he realized that he needed help.

A friend suggested that he come to a meeting with a group of men at the downtown Pittsburgh YMCA. Most of them, he discovered, were quite accomplished professionals: the CEO of a brokerage firm, the head of sales for a steel company, the city's public safety director.

"These were not like any church types I'd been around previously," Roy said. "They did not hesitate to be vulnerable. After listening for several weeks, I worked up enough courage to tell my own story. I remember one of them yelling quite loudly from down the table, 'Congratulations, now you know you need a Savior.' That was exactly the truth. I had joined a bunch of guys who understood that.

"All the other men in this group were quite a bit older. After a couple years, Paul Everett came in, introduced himself to me, and asked if I might know one other person who could start a new group with him and me. So we started praying about that.

"I was a financial officer at Mellon Bank at the time, and we were arguing over whether to keep a particular service. I felt it should be eliminated. As I walked to the elevator with the guy who was defending it, I had the overwhelming sense that he was the guy I should be asking to meet with him. I asked if he had heard of the Pittsburgh Experiment, and he said he listened to its radio program every week. So I invited him to lunch. We started meeting on Fridays at the Chinatown Inn, and he literally brought the whole Mellon Bank R&D division. That formed the nucleus of a new group of younger men, many of whom would become leaders in the Experiment over the next generation."

The Experiment group supported Roy through befriending an irascible boss (who eventually promoted Roy to senior financial officer) and then through his dismissal in 1987 after Mellon changed CEOs. When the job search wasn't going well and Roy thought he might have to relocate, he had lunch with Everett, who told him, "I know what the problem is. You're having a problem with trust." Roy was initially irked but realized, on reflection, that he needed to abandon himself more fully to God's will.

The following Monday, Roy received a call from a director of the Federal Home Loan Bank of Pittsburgh, informing him that their president/CEO position was open. Speechless, Roy wondered how the director even knew he was available. "I was fly-fishing in Wyoming for the last several weeks," the caller replied. "I've been reading back issues of the *Wall Street Journal* and I just read the article on your termination." Roy got the job and spent the next 18 years there as the bank grew to become one of the largest financial institutions in Pennsylvania. To Roy, none of that would have happened without Everett's challenge to deepen his trust.

Other than his own testimony, Roy's favorite story from his Experiment years involved a traveling salesman who requested prayer regarding his temptation to chase women while out of town. On one such night, the man was sitting in a bar, plotting a strategy to initiate a conversation with two women, when he was nudged from behind. An elder from his home church had walked into the bar and recognized him. To the salesman, it was God's angel answering the group's prayer. "He never had that problem again," Roy said, "because he would remember the angel who sat next to him at the bar."

Tom Petro's life disintegrated in sorrow when his mother died during his sophomore year of high school. He graduated only because he was such a troublemaker that the school wanted him gone despite his D average. By then he was living with members of his rock band and using fake identification to buy and consume large quantities of alcohol.

Petro didn't last long at college but got an entry-level job at Mellon Bank. Six weeks later, the person who had gotten him the job invited him to lunch with "a great group of people." Like other newcomers, Petro was attracted by the laughter, openness, and vulnerability. "Importantly for me," he added, "they didn't self-identify as a Christian group. If they had, I would have run away and never come back."

Magnetized by the Experimenters' unconditional love, Petro kept coming—for three years—before he finally committed his life to Christ. "I would not have gotten there through evangelical proclamation, because I had already predetermined that I wasn't going to find answers there," he said. "These guys never prejudged the answer; they simply were the answer in my life, loving me to the foot of the cross."

Finding Christ didn't solve all Petro's problems, however. By this point he was married, and his wife, Kris Messner, resented the fact that he shared his life more openly with a men's group than with her.

Messner agreed to go to an Experiment couples conference with him. It had four sessions, each of which contained teaching by Everett, a personal testimony by a couple (with typical Experiment vulnerability), small-group discussion, and time for each couple to spend alone.

"Two things happened that saved our marriage," Petro explained. "First, we learned from the other couples that what we were going through wasn't unusual and that we could survive it. Second, since we were both take-charge leaders trying to run everything, an older woman told us to divide up our responsibilities and pick where I would lead and where Kris would lead. That simple advice has worked for 32 years since then. We would not have gotten that guidance, or been open to it, if not for the Experiment and the hope that it provided us."

Messner later helped to found one of the Experiment's first mixed-gender groups. In 1989, the couple moved to eastern Pennsylvania, where Petro led two successful turnarounds of failing banks. Dick Bauer, who hired him away from Mellon and then served on the board of directors at one of the banks Petro turned around, testified to the extent to which Petro's transformation through the Experiment shaped his business leadership.

"Tom started every board meeting with prayer," Bauer recalled. "I have been on a lot of boards and saw that maybe once or twice, but not in a for-profit situation. I saw how he treated his people, and his Christian faith was displayed in many ways—his core values, style, and integrity. I watched him in his dealings with other companies and saw the same decency and respect." Petro also became a Bible teacher and key leader at his church and a board member at Eastern University in Philadelphia. All this was possible because a few caring men in downtown Pittsburgh refused to be put off by his tough shell.

"They called me their M&M," Petro said of his Experiment colleagues—"hard on the outside, but soft and chewy on the inside."

A story published in the January-February 1964 *Faith at Work* magazine fascinatingly depicted the boldness and generosity of three of the Experiment's most cherished early leaders:

> Bob Brooks, an unemployed insurance debit man, was leaving a meeting of Employment Anonymous at the Downtown YMCA with Kirwan Flannery. As they walked along Wood Street, Bob

noticed a sign announcing a creative writing course, starting the next evening at the Y, and remarked that writing was his life ambition. He knew he had an aptitude for it, but no schooling. He expressed a strong desire to attend this course, but said it was impossible both financially and because it was too late to sign up. Kirwan asked him if he had prayed about it and Bob answered that he hadn't had time because he had just seen the sign. Kirwan suggested they try an experiment in prayer.

At Fourth and Wood Streets they ran into Dick Durstein and told him of Bob's desire to enter the writing course. Dick had never met Bob, but without hesitation, he took his name and said he would do some checking and call Bob in an hour. And Dick walked on.

Bob said, "Why would he do that for me, a total stranger?" Kirwan explained that he and Dick shared a Christian life and this made them free to be honest with one another. "This honesty," Bob said, "is what I have been looking for all my life. How do you get it?"

They continued down Wood Street discussing honesty and the subject of forgiveness for the past came up. Kirwan was not sure he could help Bob too much and sent up a quick prayer for help. As the two of them waited at the corner of Fifth and Wood for the light to change, Kirk Cunningham appeared and the three of them started to talk about forgiveness. Within a few minutes, Kirk gave the clearest and most easily understood analogy of forgiveness that either Kirwan or Bob had ever heard.

Then a miracle really happened. On the busiest corner in Pittsburgh where crowds of people pass, the three men prayed together asking God's forgiveness, Bob committing his life to Christ and Kirk and Kirwan recommitting theirs.

An hour later, Dick called Bob to say that some men were raising the money to pay for the writer's course, and that he had talked to a board member of the Y and they were making room for him. Thus in a few minutes help came—theological, material and spiritual—in answer to a simple prayer.

THE VALUE OF A SOFT SELL

The stories of lives dramatically changed by the Experiment illustrate how its low-key approach melted hard exteriors and enabled spiritually needy people to welcome Christ into their hearts. Some outsiders felt that the approach was insufficiently evangelistic or questioned the Experiment's lack of attention to Bible study. But as Purcell and Petro's narratives indicate, this method reached people who would have not responded to a more overtly Christian initial invitation.

Moreover, the depth of personal sharing that took place routinely at Experiment meetings could not have happened if the sessions had included Bible studies—there simply would not have been enough time.

"There are a lot of ministries that cater to Christians," said Ted Kerr, a financial advisor who served as the Experiment's part-time executive director from 2012 to 2017. "When I hear some pastors preach, I feel they don't really understand what it feels like to be completely lost. All our executive directors have understood that. It puts us in a unique position to serve as Christians in society. We grab people who are walking blindly."

Indeed, the Experiment has been led almost without interruption by adult converts who were successful in business yet suffered acutely from emptiness of heart. The carousing Don James was the prototype, but Offill, Everett, former Mellon banker Carter Birely, Fraas, and Kerr all fit the pattern as well.

Kerr also emphasized the need for organizations like the Experiment that can connect with people through unmistakable acts of interpersonal caring that open doors for the gospel message. "Ultimately, proclamation is essential in calling people to confession and profession of faith," he stated, "but demonstrating one's faith is also a completely valid way of sharing Christ in the world. The Experiment specializes in demonstration, primarily through nonjudgmental listening and prayer."

THE CULTURE HAS CHANGED, BUT THE NEED REMAINS

By the 1990s, the Experiment model was struggling. Changes in the marketplace and in Pittsburgh's economy had greatly reduced the concentration of jobs in large companies or in the city's compact Golden Triangle, making recruitment more difficult. In one sense, the Experiment was a victim of its own success, as close-knit small groups had become an established feature of many congregations.

Birely, the last executive director to have strong personal fundraising connections, retired in 2009 due to health difficulties. On the day when he was to meet with successor Kerry Fraas to discuss the donor list, Birely suffered a severe stroke that sharply limited his capacities for the remainder of his life.

With the number of weekly Experiment groups having dwindled from 40 in its heyday to just a handful, Fraas expected to be the organization's last executive director, but Kerr persuaded the board not to close the doors. Instead, the organization celebrated its 60th anniversary in 2015 by adopting a new "Skyline Vision" of planting groups in each of the city's 25 tallest office buildings. In 2017, the Experiment once again hired a full-time executive, former Young Life leader Chris Buda. As of September 2018, he had built the number of Experiment groups back up to 16—five downtown and 11 in the surrounding suburbs.

"Today people can be more connected than ever, but there are more people in counseling than ever before, and the chief complaint is loneliness," Buda commented. "They need relationships." Buda believes that the Experiment's approach is well suited for unchurched millennials, and that the organization can continue to thrive if it equips believers to "stand by the door" and make meaningful, nonthreatening connections with unbelievers in an increasingly non-Christian culture.

Tom Petro agreed emphatically that the Experiment's work is not done. "Millennials whose view of the church has been shaped by sex and financial scandals are still on a spiritual quest," he said. "If there is any ministry fundamentally equipped to stand by the door and help people find the latch, it is the Experiment. It is as relevant today as when Sam founded it."

Four

IT ALL STARTED HERE:
THE BIRTH OF CATHOLIC CHARISMATIC RENEWAL

It was February 1967. The Catholic Church was experiencing a historic period of change as it reacted to the new openness dramatically ushered in by the Second Vatican Council of 1962–1965. Use of the vernacular rather than Latin in worship, greater concern for lay education and involvement, and early steps toward broader ecumenical engagement had created new opportunities for Catholics to pursue personal spiritual development and interact with other Christian streams.

In this evolving environment, 25 students attending Duquesne University in Pittsburgh, members of a campus group intended to promote spiritual growth and social action, went on a weekend retreat with two faculty members and a university chaplain. They did not expect their roughly 40 hours together to be reported even in the campus newspaper, let alone worldwide.

What happened during those three days at the Ark and the Dove retreat center in Gibsonia, north of Pittsburgh, is universally recognized as the birth of the Catholic charismatic renewal, which has grown to an estimated 120 million adherents, reshaped the Catholic Church to the extent that observers often refer to its "charismatic wing," and greatly influenced relations between Catholics and other Christians.

Unlike all the other stories contained in this book, the story of the Duquesne Weekend of February 17–19, 1967 and its aftermath has already been well told. Many historians have recounted it, and original participant Patti Gallagher Mansfield has definitively described the event in her book *As by a New Pentecost*, which contains firsthand testimonies from about half of those who attended. To go beyond a simple rehash, in this chapter we summarize the historic retreat (adding one significant source, previously unpublished in English) and then describe the ongoing spread and impact of charismatic renewal in Pittsburgh. That latter part of the story is largely overlooked because the driving force behind the movement shifted from Pittsburgh to other places almost immediately after the initial outbreak.

A HOLY CURIOSITY REWARDED

The charismatic movement in mainline Christian denominations—characterized by joyful and expressive worship, speaking in tongues, messages of prophecy, and healing ministries—was long preceded by its half-sister of sorts: the Pentecostal movement, the birth of which most historians place in 1901. Pentecostals were a culturally marginalized group for decades but gained greater respectability by the 1950s, aided by the Full Gospel Business Men's Fellowship International (which brought Pentecostal worship into hotel ballrooms) and the success of Pentecostal preachers like Oral Roberts.

Over time, many individual Christians from non-Pentecostal denominations had their own Pentecostal experience, usually described as a "baptism in the Spirit" accompanied by great spiritual fervor and often by speaking in tongues. These believers began to spread the Pentecostal message quietly in their own churches.

The first prominent instance of a denominational leader embracing such practices occurred in 1960, when Dennis Bennett, associate pastor of an Episcopal church in Van Nuys, California, announced during a sermon that he had spoken in tongues. A fellow pastor walked out in protest and Bennett was soon reassigned to a struggling parish in Seattle, where major charismatic revival ensued.

Similar events took place in other Protestant denominations during the 1960s, leading to the creation of charismatic organizations within each mainline denomination that held conferences and built extensive networks of adherents. For the most part, the denominations themselves expressed cautious approval of this source of spiritual inspiration.

Thus, when two Catholic university instructors wanted to inquire into such practices in 1966, they didn't have to wander into a Pentecostal church with a worship style far discrepant from their own liturgical and devotional lives; instead they could drop in on a prayer group of respectable, mature Protestant denominational charismatics in suburban Pittsburgh.

Mansfield's book highlights several factors that converged to bring the two Duquesne faculty members (theology instructor Ralph Keifer and history instructor Bill Storey) to this point. Both were active in the Cursillo movement, founded in Spain and transplanted to the United States in the late 1950s, which sought to introduce Catholics to deeper encounters with God through intense three-day retreats and follow-up reunions. Through this involvement, they were acquainted with fellow *cursillistas* at the University of Notre Dame and with national Cursillo leaders Ralph Martin and Steve Clark, who were based at Michigan State University's student parish.

In 1966, two classic Pentecostal books slipped into this circle of revival-focused Catholics. One was *The Cross and the Switchblade*, Pentecostal preacher David Wilkerson's 1963 story of his Spirit-inspired work with drug addicts and gang members in New York City. The other was *They Speak with Other Tongues* (1964) by John Sherrill, an editor for Norman Vincent Peale's *Guideposts* magazine who set out to investigate the phenomenon of speaking in tongues and ended up having a Pentecostal experience himself. According to Mansfield, Clark received Wilkerson's book from an evangelical student ministry worker at Michigan State and Sherrill's book from a Notre Dame graduate who had visited a Pentecostal church with a friend in Toronto.

At a national Cursillo convention in August 1966, Clark gave copies of these two books to Keifer and Storey. The two men read Wilkerson's book and were provoked to investigate scriptural teaching on the work of the Holy Spirit. What they discovered, according to Kevin and Dorothy Ranaghan's retelling in their 1969 book *Catholic Pentecostals*, was like "discovering Christianity for the first time."

By November, Keifer and Storey had resolved to look for someone who they felt could lead them to a fuller understanding of this Pentecostal experience. Of course, there were no fellow Catholics to guide them. They consulted with an Episcopal priest who had delivered a lecture at Duquesne, and he referred them to Betty Schomaker, a member of his parish who attended a charismatic prayer group hosted by a Presbyterian woman, Flo Dodge.

On January 13, 1967, Keifer with wife Bobbi, Storey, and Duquesne theology instructor Patrick Bourgeois attended Dodge's prayer group. According to Mansfield, Storey requested prayer for baptism in the Holy Spirit that evening and the group prayed for him; he did not speak in tongues at that time, but those present indicated a strong sense of God's power and presence.

On January 20, Keifer and Bourgeois attended again and both received the gift of tongues as others prayed with them. (In fact, Bourgeois would later refer to this date as the actual beginning of the Catholic charismatic renewal.) During the following week, Keifer's wife also spoke in tongues.

A lengthy letter that Keifer wrote to a friend on February 11, 1967, reprinted in Mansfield's book, shows that he was already engaging in theological reflection so as to interpret his new experience within a Catholic context. (Mansfield did not identify the letter's original recipient, but it was presumably Steve Clark, since Keifer thanked him "for starting me on the path to all this.") Keifer affirmed that the prayer group's beliefs were consistent with Catholic understanding, related baptism in the Spirit to Catholic sacramental theology, and described with delight the ecumenical unity he was experiencing. He also presciently anticipated the challenge of introducing fellow Catholics to his experience while retaining them within the Catholic Church. "It is well to remember," Keifer wrote frankly, "that to many Pentecostals and Evangelicals, we represent at best a dead institutionalism, and at worst the Anti-Christ. Unless they know and respect real Catholics, they will not direct fringe Catholics back to their own Church."

THE DUQUESNE WEEKEND: IMPERFECTLY PRIMED, SPONTANEOUSLY JOYFUL

Keifer and Storey had an ideal pilot group to work with: 25 young, devout members of Duquesne's Chi Rho society, formed to provide an alternative to Greek life for Catholic students with a strong interest in spiritual development and social action. The two faculty, who served as advisors to the group, had intended to use Jesus' Sermon on the Mount as the scriptural focus for the group's February 17–19 retreat. Based on their January experiences, they changed their plans and instead asked the students to read the first four chapters of the book of Acts and *The Cross and the Switchblade* in preparation for the retreat.

The Ark (the main building of the Ark and the Dove retreat center, where the Catholic charismatic renewal was born) in 2016.

In view of this assignment, it would not be fully accurate to say that the Chi Rho students were totally unprepared for what would happen that weekend. But neither were they directly coached toward a particular type of emotional experience. Mansfield, for example, read Wilkerson's book and was deeply impressed by his sense of knowing God's will but overlooked the references to baptism in the Spirit and speaking in tongues. David Mangan, another student at the center of the retreat's historic moments, wrote that when he read the book those references "all went over my head. After reading it I still had no idea what speaking in tongues was all about."

During the retreat, according to Mansfield's notes, one of the faculty advisors asked the students, "Are you ready for what the Spirit may do to you?" They appear to have made no suggestion that the Spirit should be manifested to the students in the form of particular gifts. However, Betty Schomaker delivered the talk on the Pentecost account in Acts 2 and, according to David Mangan, told the group, "This is still happening today." Paul Gray, a recent Duquesne graduate who had presented the message on Acts 1, said that Schomaker's words "gave us a hunger for the reality of Pentecost in our lives."

On Saturday night, February 18, a birthday party for several students was on the schedule. Mansfield went into the chapel to tell any students located there to come downstairs for the party. She knelt as Catholics traditionally do when in the presence of the sacrament. As she did so, she wrote later, "my body literally trembled before [God's] majesty and holiness." Chi Rho president Bill Deigan entered the chapel and knelt next to her. When Mansfield told him what she was experiencing, Deigan indicated that others were also having unusually powerful experiences and encouraged her to keep praying.

Mansfield offered the Lord a prayer of surrender. Her testimony describes what happened next:

> The next moment I found myself prostrate, flat on my face, stretched out before the tabernacle. No one had laid hands on me. I had never seen such a thing happen before. I don't know exactly how it took

place, but in the process, my shoes came off my feet. Later I realized that, like Moses before the burning bush, I was indeed upon holy ground. As I lay there, I was flooded from my fingertips to my toes with a deep sense of God's personal love for me.

Mansfield reported her experience to chaplain Joseph Healy, who told her that much the same thing had happened to David Mangan in the chapel a short time earlier. Indeed, according to his testimony, Mangan had fallen prostrate under the power of God twice while entering the chapel and felt an urge to pray in a language other than English, which he began to do after the faculty advisors assured him that praying in tongues was scriptural.

Mansfield invited others to the chapel and about a dozen had similar experiences—some weeping, some laughing, some feeling a tingling in their throats, and some spontaneously, without instruction, praying in tongues. Many of the students remained together, overcome by praise and rejoicing, until the early morning hours.

The only extant photo of the whole group who attended the Duquesne Weekend, except for John Rossmiller who took the picture. Patti Mansfield and David Mangan are at the front left.

THE NEWS SPREADS

Those who had been supernaturally touched on the Duquesne Weekend came back to campus and told others. Their message was not always well received. Mansfield's roommate questioned her mental stability. Chaplain Healy, concerned about the fledgling charismatics' potential for emotionalism, soon distanced himself from their activities. The Chi Rho group was split internally between enthusiastic supporters and skeptics of Pentecostal-style renewal, and the charismatic members' prayer meetings soon moved off campus to the residences of Keifer and then Bourgeois.

Storey's maturity helped to avert sensationalistic media attention that could have generated backlash against the movement. When *Time* magazine heard about the tongue speakers at Duquesne and sought to cover the story, the response was that "we don't want the publicity," and no report was published. The students had such utter respect for Storey that they followed his lead faithfully in this matter.

Keifer, the more overt of the two on the initial retreat, also was cautious about his public pronouncements. John Sweeney completed his undergraduate studies at Duquesne in 1969 without ever hearing about the Duquesne Weekend. He took a course from Keifer in spring 1967 and said that the instructor made no reference to his charismatic experience, "but I remember him vividly as having a kind of glow when he talked about theology and his faith." Only after Sweeney entered the charismatic renewal himself in 1975, after several years as a priest, did he learn that Keifer had been there at the beginning.

However, accounts of the outpouring of February 18 received an enthusiastic response from Keifer and Storey's network of renewal-oriented peers. Two weekends later, Storey visited Notre Dame and met with about 30 interested people, some of whom prayed with him to receive baptism in the Spirit. On March 13, many of these met with the local Full Gospel Business Men's president and Pentecostal ministers, becoming the first Catholics to pray in tongues alongside Pentecostals while declaring that they intended to remain within the Catholic Church.

Within weeks, charismatic prayer meetings began at Notre Dame, one of America's most prominent Catholic institutions.

Martin and Clark came to Pittsburgh to visit the impacted students, prayed with Keifer and Storey, and took the charismatic message of renewal through baptism in the Spirit back with them to Michigan. In April, they and about 40 Michigan State students—including a defensive lineman who had played against Notre Dame the previous November in college football's "Game of the Century"—joined 40 from Notre Dame for a charismatic retreat that garnered national publicity.

During the Notre Dame summer session, which attracts Catholics from across the country, several of the Catholic charismatics decided to hold a panel discussion on the Pentecostal movement. Forty attenders expressed interest in coming to a prayer meeting. "We divided them into two groups of 20 and invited one group to come Wednesday and the other on Saturday," the Ranaghans wrote in *Catholic Pentecostals*. "When we reached the meeting place the first Wednesday expecting to find 20 people, we found about 150 priests, seminarians, nuns, and lay people assembled. … It was like that twice a week for three weeks." Many of those who experienced these meetings started similar groups in their home areas across the United States, and a national movement was off and running.

The U.S. Catholic Bishops' Committee on Doctrine examined Catholic charismatic renewal in 1969, concluding that "the movement should at this point not be inhibited but allowed to develop." Four books by respected Catholics, all published between 1969 and 1971, added further credibility and theological substance to what charismatic Catholics were doing. With the bishops' cautious endorsement, Catholic charismatic leaders were free to offer their pathway to spiritual reinvigoration all over the country. When Mansfield attended her first Catholic charismatic conference at Notre Dame in fall 1967, there were 50 participants; in 1973, there were 35,000.

A FOUNDER'S LATER RECOLLECTION

Consistent with the university's hands-off attitude toward the charismatic renewal, the Duquesne archives on the topic are sparse. However, they do contain one item of considerable historical value: a handwritten recollection attributed to William G. Storey, dated January 1994 and apparently prepared at the request of a Duquesne professor writing a history of the university. As Storey had disassociated himself from the charismatic movement by the mid-1970s, his version, though his memory of some minor details appears to have been clouded by the passage of time, serves as a valuable independent confirmation of the essential facts. To the best of our knowledge, it has never been published previously in English (although a translation appears in a Spanish-language book on the charismatic renewal).

Storey explained that his interest in Pentecostalism was sparked by four factors: his belief that Catholic liturgy was "in desperate need of a thorough revitalization," his enthusiasm for the reforms initiated by Vatican II, his sense that the U.S. Catholic bishops were not providing sufficiently bold leadership in implementing those reforms, and his strong ecumenical conviction that all Christian churches should learn from each other. He then continued:

> As a result, when through the influence of friends whom I respected in the Cursillo movement I did some rather superficial reading in the history and styles of 20th-century Protestant Pentecostalism, in company with another Duquesne professor, Ralph Keifer, we decided to attend the house church worship of a Mrs. Dodge in the North Hills of Pittsburgh and experience firsthand the forms of worship of current Pentecostalism. We did this after interviewing Mrs. Dodge's Anglican pastor (Father Lewis) on January 6, 1967. [Storey here misidentified Dodge as the woman from Lewis's parish.] When he assured us of the background and style of the leader of that prayer group, three of us attended our first meeting on January 13 in Mrs. Dodge's living room. The three were Ralph Keifer, his wife Bobbi, and I. My wife expressed no interest in such goings-on and was unfazed by and even hostile to our subsequent involvement.

The first meeting interested me because of its warm and friendly atmosphere, its apparent spontaneity, its peculiar forms of prayer (speaking in tongues, prophecy and interpretation, and fervent intercessory prayer) and its leadership by a woman.

The three of us returned the following week. Bobbi and Ralph were prayed over by the group and received the gift of tongues as a sign of their fuller entry into the Holy Spirit. I did not receive such a "gift" either then or later but was impressed and edified by their experience and willing to learn more. I believe it was also on that occasion that Patrick Bourgeois, a Duquesne philosophy professor, was present and spoke in tongues.

Since our "hearts were strangely warmed," as John Wesley put it, by these new experiences we decided to continue to seek God in these Pentecostal ways and see what flowed from them.

Just before the Christmas vacation Ralph and I had engaged the Ark and the Dove, a Roman Catholic retreat house in the North Hills, for a weekend for ourselves and several students who belonged to a scripture study and prayer group called the Chi Rho Society. Given our recent Pentecostal contacts, we decided to lay aside the received agenda and concentrate instead on the early chapters of the Acts of the Apostles and their possible spiritual and liturgical connections with Pentecostalism.

As neophytes ourselves, this was both premature and presumptuous of us but we proceeded in all innocence to pick student speakers to lead discussion of various aspects of Acts and to arrange our forms of morning and evening prayer and the masses that were to be celebrated by our beloved and fervent chaplain, Father Joseph Healy, C.S.Sp.

The retreat began Friday evening, February 17 and was to run all day Saturday and most of Sunday. Our carefully thought-out schedule fell to pieces as soon as we began Friday evening when people began deserting the opening "party" for the chapel of the Ark and the Dove where a pandemonium broke loose at once and lasted far into the night. [All other sources place this activity on Saturday night.] Spontaneous Scripture reading, spontaneous prayer, ecstatic utterances, tongue speaking, tears, laughter, and prostrations overflowed from the chapel into the rooms and few people got much sleep that night. The following day was joyful, exciting and a little disturbing. I was more a passive participant than Ralph who took it upon himself to "exorcise" some difficult cases and so to increase the level of enthusiasm in the students. By Sunday morning I was deeply moved and puzzled by the spiritual experiences all around me and I did not feel entitled to discourage or clamp down on them. Rather I fell into a kind of holy stupor myself, particularly after a moving mass celebrated by Father Healy. Even though one or two students asked me to intervene and put a stop to some of the more vivid occurrences, I couldn't find the resources to do so and the retreat ended in a blur of happy confusion.

So unusual was the weekend that on Monday morning I had the presence of mind to call our bishop [John Wright] to inform him what had happened. He was at a meeting in another city but came immediately to the phone and listened attentively but practically without comment as I presented him with a succinct report. Later I learned he then spoke to the nuns who operated the Ark and the Dove and got their side of the story. Subsequently Bishop Wright avoided ever mentioning the Ark and the Dove weekend to me and I had only one exchange with him on the subject of "Catholic charismatics" at a much later date when he was a curial cardinal.

The weeks that followed February 17–19 were filled with discussion, prayer meetings and consultations with friends and enemies of the Pentecostal outburst.

By a strange coincidence both Ralph and I visited Notre Dame in the following few weeks, Ralph to take a teaching position at St. Mary's College and to enter the doctoral program in liturgical studies and I—to my considerable surprise—to be interviewed at Notre Dame as a prospective professor of liturgy and church history. As it happened, both Ralph and I had former students and friends at Notre Dame who had already heard rumors of the Duquesne events and were dying to hear more. Most of them were already well primed for further spiritual developments by previous participation in the Cursillo and by regular attendance at Scripture study groups.

Both Ralph and I were imprudent enough to blurt out all we had heard and seen since January 6, so that by mid-April a Pentecostal explosion had begun at Notre Dame.

WHAT STARTED IN PITTSBURGH CONTINUED IN PITTSBURGH

Both Keifer and Storey accepted positions in South Bend and relocated in summer 1967, leaving their charismatic disciples in Pittsburgh leaderless. Partly for this reason, the movement's center of gravity decisively shifted elsewhere, and published histories give no further attention to activities at the point of origin. But what happened beyond summer 1967 in Pittsburgh still makes an interesting and instructive tale.

In place of Keifer and Storey, the still-small group of charismatic Catholics selected David Mangan, a 1966 Duquesne graduate and thus one of the older students on the retreat, as its leader. Mangan and several others spent part of the summer living with charismatic Lutheran pastor Harald Bredesen in Mount Vernon, New York, being mentored by him while doing evangelistic outreach.

In fall 1967, the group began holding prayer meetings on Mount Washington and then at a church on Pittsburgh's South Side. Storey's immediate post-retreat interaction with Bishop Wright bore fruit as the charismatics received permission to operate, rather than opposition, from diocesan leadership. In 1968 they outgrew their meeting room and moved to an Episcopal church in the city's Hazelwood neighborhood.

From the beginning, the renewal was ecumenical in nature, bringing

Catholics and non-Catholics together for praise and fellowship. That feature produced tensions along with joy, as the Catholic participants regularly encountered Protestant charismatics who expected their newly Spirit-inspired friends to see the light and leave the Catholic Church.

"We always had people coming from other churches, sometimes to see if we were for real," Mangan recalled. "It was tricky to be respectful while not giving people a forum to evangelize Catholics." Mangan said that many visitors used the technique of inserting Scripture lessons within their prayers: "Lord, as you know it says in [a Bible verse that they thought Catholics needed to hear] … ." Mangan would walk over to such people and say gently, "You are praying nicely, but please give others a turn."

Mangan quickly became adept at handling potentially sensitive situations, such as when the group recited the Lord's Prayer and some Protestants kept going where Catholics stop (traditionally, Catholics do not say the line beginning "For thine is the kingdom"). Sometimes a Catholic participant would return the favor by reciting the Hail Mary prayer (which Protestants do not use because of their differing view of Mary's role).

The renewal in Pittsburgh spread exponentially as people attended the main charismatic gathering and then launched prayer groups in their own parishes. Within a few years there were 60 such groups, ranging in size from a dozen people to several hundred weekly participants. According to Mangan, the growth took place too rapidly and haphazardly to be traced: "People would do prayer meeting hopping, visiting different sites to see what they liked and then starting their own."

In addition to raising issues of theological and pastoral fidelity, the explosive growth sometimes spawned an undertone of rivalry between groups. After his return from a Peace Corps assignment in Turkey in 1968, Tom Mangan (David's brother) helped to organize monthly meetings of prayer group leaders, which gradually softened the impulse toward rivalry and also enabled participants to learn from each other and discuss common challenges.

The growing renewal movement appointed one of Pittsburgh's first charismatic priests, Ed Bunchek, as liaison to the diocese. That connection helped to assure diocesan leadership that the movement would remain loyal to the Catholic Church.

Tom Mangan believed that five or six regional prayer gatherings would have been better than 60 separate groups of varying strength and leadership quality, but others did not want to give up their parish-based prayer groups. Instead, the main vehicle creating consistency of instruction was the Life in the Spirit Seminars, an initiatory curriculum that Ralph Martin and Steve Clark began developing within the first year of their charismatic activity and published in a seven-week format by 1971. This tool enabled group leaders, rather than simply praying over people who sought baptism in the Spirit, to introduce charismatic spirituality in a broader theological context and with greater preparation.

Despite the leaders' best efforts, there were always outliers, like the troubled man who declared, at one prayer meeting where Tom Mangan was presiding, that he was the new John the Baptist. "When you turn the light on," Tom observed, "you get people's attention, but you also attract bugs." In response to such episodes, the initial openness to anyone inspired to speak forth a "word from the Lord" was replaced by the establishment of "discernment teams" who would determine whether a participant's message should be shared with the full meeting.

The use of seven-week seminars also helped to balance the pursuit of intense emotional experience with the fostering of longer-term relationships. "Many people would come for a year and then leave," Tom Mangan explained. "Rather than just being a spiritual filling station, we tried to build community so that people would stay around."

Community building took two main forms. Many of the local prayer groups became closely connected to their parishes, gaining relational stability but losing their ecumenical flavor. On the other hand, Martin and Clark, after losing their jobs in East Lansing due to their charismatic involvement, moved to Ann Arbor and founded the Word of God ecumenical covenant community, which grew to 1,000 members and became

David and Tom Mangan at a People of God Community men's breakfast, September 2018. David was the guest speaker.

a major spiritual force locally and nationally. The word *covenant* highlighted the expectation of a long-term, often permanent commitment to the community and its members. In the Pittsburgh area, covenant groups formed in the north and west suburbs and eventually merged as the People of God, which continues to function today in the Coraopolis area with about 150 members. The People of God avoided the serious charges of authoritarian control and emotional abuse that rocked the covenant communities in Ann Arbor, South Bend, and elsewhere as early as the mid-1970s, with Storey among the leading critics.

STILL GOING STRONG AT 50

As the renewal became institutionalized within Pittsburgh-area Catholic parishes, it received significant infusions from Franciscan University of Steubenville, Ohio, which became one of the nation's leading bastions of Catholic charismatic activity under president Michael Scanlan. For example, Father John Sweeney's involvement was nurtured by Franciscan

University prayer meetings while he was serving a parish in Burgettstown, Pa., 17 miles east of Steubenville. Sweeney attended the Life in the Spirit Seminars in 1975 and has been a charismatic voice within the Diocese of Pittsburgh for more than 40 years. Scanlan was a cofounder of and regular speaker at the charismatic-oriented FIRE rallies (faith, intercession, repentance, evangelism) that spread worldwide; one of the first such rallies attracted thousands of Catholics to the Monroeville Expo Mart in 1985.

Russ Bixler, who would later found Pittsburgh's Christian television station, organized major summer charismatic conferences during the 1980s. Those annual events were hosted (though certainly not sponsored) by Duquesne and included substantial Catholic participation.

At the international level, Belgian Cardinal Leon Joseph Suenens's early embrace of the charismatic renewal was crucial, leading to support from Pope Paul VI. In 1975, a large Catholic charismatic assembly took place in Rome; every pope since then has been supportive. Patti Mansfield, just a spiritually searching undergraduate student in 1967, worshiped alongside Pope Francis on Pentecost Sunday (June 4), 2017 as he celebrated the movement's golden jubilee.

Pope Francis and Patti Mansfield at the golden jubilee celebration of the Catholic charismatic renewal in Rome, June 4, 2017.

The once-flourishing weekly prayer groups have declined—"probably because of the pace of life today," Sweeney said—but Catholics with charismatic experience continue to be active and effective contributors to their parishes, and a fraternity of charismatic priests within the Pittsburgh diocese has been meeting weekly for 25 years.

Catholics in Pittsburgh also had something special to celebrate as the renewal's 50-year anniversary approached. In December 2015, the National Service Committee of the Catholic Charismatic Renewal (NSC) purchased the Ark and the Dove retreat center. It had passed from the diocese to the Sisters of Divine Providence. When they decided to sell it, Tom Mangan organized an effort to develop a bid, the NSC committed a down payment, and an anonymous donor put up the rest of the money. Mangan and his colleagues formed a separate nonprofit to make the project more ecumenical. "We don't want to be a charismatic museum piece, but a catalyst for moving things forward for the next 50 years," he said.

The NSC marked the renewal's 50th anniversary in February 2017 with a national leaders' conference, attended by 120 people, that included field trips to the Ark and the Dove. When the NSC held its jubilee conference in Pittsburgh that July, demand to visit the movement's birthplace among the 6,200 participants was overwhelming.

The retreat center has not yet matched Lourdes in popularity as a pilgrimage site, but if you visit the Ark and the Dove and feel something unusual as you walk into the chapel, you won't be the first.

LASTING LESSONS

Many who have studied tongue speaking have viewed the phenomenon as psychologically induced rather than as a gift from God. The approach to receiving tongues typically applied by both classical Pentecostalism and the Life in the Spirit Seminars could reinforce that interpretation, as the instruction encourages participants to speak out in a new language when leaders pray over them. However, the testimonies of the Duquesne students are not easily explained away as psychological manipulation. The students consistently indicated that they did not expect to speak in tongues, and most of their initial, spontaneous experiences of an overwhelming spiritual presence did not involve tongues.

Based on the available evidence, it is hard to deny a supernatural influence in the events of February 18, 1967, or in the overall ripple effects of this outpouring. Certainly the charismatic movement has had some serious wrong turns, but the original impulse has unleashed deep joy and faithfulness in millions of Catholic and other Christians.

The apostle Paul argued that God does not work primarily through the rich and powerful, but that he chooses the foolish and weak to shame the wise and strong (1 Corinthians 1:27). The Duquesne students had no claim to fame, spiritual maturity, or connections. Some of them were questioning their own faith. But they opened themselves up transparently to God's work in their life, and God worked through them in amazing ways.

At the same time, few would have believed the testimonies of a dozen young students telling what had happened to them and urging the Catholic world to seek after the same thing. The essential ingredient that caused the initial reports of the Duquesne Weekend to be taken seriously elsewhere was Keifer and Storey's credibility, which opened doors in many places where others trusted their judgment. Great spiritual fervor cannot become a renewing current of grace unless it flows within the channels established by Scripture, credible authority, and tradition.

A bitter irony in this story highlights the fact that emotional experience—even one that becomes world-changing—cannot by itself sustain an individual's walk with God. Both Keifer and Storey followed other paths in their later lives, to such an extent that Mansfield, while emphasizing the "debt of gratitude" that the movement owes to those two instructors, never identifies them by name.

On the other hand, for Mansfield, David Mangan, and others who were prepared to become "fools for Christ," February 18, 1967 remains the defining day of their lives. Speaking at a men's breakfast in suburban Pittsburgh in September 2018, David joked that he had aged to the point where "I get tired just saying the word *zeal*," but his total commitment to

Christ had not changed. "Are you willing to try anything for Jesus, as long as you know it is him?" he challenged his listeners.

The original retreat participants' willingness to tell of what happened to them and to reproduce it in other lives has made the Duquesne Weekend the source of arguably the greatest spiritual force ever to come out of Pittsburgh.

Five

THE MASTER CONNECTOR AND HIS WEB OF INFLUENCE:
REID CARPENTER, THE PITTSBURGH OFFENSIVE, THE PITTSBURGH LEADERSHIP FOUNDATION, ET AL.

Reid Carpenter reached Pittsburgh in 1961 and Sam Shoemaker left in 1962, so they had very little direct contact, but that minimal interaction was memorable.

Don James first introduced the two to each other, describing Carpenter as the new Young Life leader. Shoemaker responded, "Welcome. I've been praying for you for years."

Carpenter already revered the beloved Episcopal clergyman because of Shoemaker's friendship with Young Life founder Jim Rayburn. "Shoemaker gave Young Life public support during Young Life's struggling beginnings. He was one of the few credible clergy who stood up for us," Carpenter said.

In spring 1962, Shoemaker took James and Carpenter to a Mount Washington overlook to pray for the city of Pittsburgh. During that mountaintop prayer time, Shoemaker took on a prophet's mantle; for

Carpenter, the experience was almost a transfiguration. Shoemaker wasn't Jesus, but "it was as if Jesus himself were speaking through Sam, declaring that Pittsburgh would become a place that would bring him great honor. It was so compelling that it brought us to our knees. Even when I talk about it now, the hair on my arms stands straight up."

Shoemaker challenged this young new arrival in Pittsburgh to commit himself to and embrace a vision for this city. That call to place-based ministry in Pittsburgh would last for over 40 years, after which Carpenter went on to help Christian leaders as far away as India to do the same thing.

How did a young, rough-around-the-edges youth ministry leader end up mobilizing civic leaders and millions of dollars to transform a city? It's a long story. Happily, since the story has never before been fully told in writing—the only publication substantially devoted to Carpenter ends with the founding of the Pittsburgh Leadership Foundation in 1978—he kindly spent 20 hours telling it to us. Many others have contributed or verified information, but this chapter can be most colorfully and compellingly told as an outgrowth of what happened after one man, under the direct influence of Sam Shoemaker, committed himself to building the kingdom of God in Pittsburgh.

A SURVIVOR OF FUNDAMENTALISM

Born in 1938, Carpenter grew up attending Black Rock Congregational Church in Bridgeport, Connecticut. His mother was the daughter of Charles McDowell, who had pastored the congregation for 21 years and was primarily responsible for making it an evangelical bastion. Carpenter said he had 26 relatives in the church.

"Black Rock in those days was what one would call a fundamentalist church, with all the great and the not-so-great aspects of fundamentalism," he explained. "What saved us was that we all had each other, so we could be humorously rebellious together without getting into drugs. None of us got into serious trouble, but within that ultraconservative framework, we were on the edge."

In the early 1950s a cousin 10 years older than Carpenter, Dean Borgman, returned from the Korean War and started a cutting-edge church youth group, Black Rock Teenagers, which soon was attracting hundreds of youth. A dashing young motorcycle rider and a great speaker, Borgman reached beyond the fundamentalist culture to reach outsiders, even picking up youth in public housing to bring them to Saturday night meetings. (Borgman would go on to an illustrious career as an Episcopal priest and seminary professor; in his eighties he was still teaching youth ministry at Gordon-Conwell Seminary.)

Reid Carpenter in 2018.

"I can remember being on the back of Dean's motorcycle coming back from a Bible study, hanging on to my hero and asking myself, 'Does it get any better than this?'" Carpenter said. Black Rock Teenagers was a formative experience for him, marked by interracial fellowship, hilarity, and a sense of adventure.

"But the Christian faith hadn't really sunk into my soul," he admitted. He was incorrigible in school, flunked classes, even stole a car on a whim, and barely graduated from high school. His academic record couldn't get him accepted anywhere—except Moody Bible Institute, because his parents had influence there. Due to his immaturity and lack of serious interest in academics, Moody asked him not to return after his second year.

Carpenter returned to Connecticut and moved in with Borgman, who was just starting a local branch of Young Life, a Christian outreach to teens that featured entertaining activities, relational ministry, and summer adventure camp experiences. "I was in no spiritual shape to be leading a group," Carpenter said, "but I could share other responsibilities under Dean's leadership."

In 1957, as Borgman and Harv Oostdyk initiated Young Life work in New York City, Carpenter had "the privilege of living on the Lower East

Side, riding motorcycles, and infiltrating gangs." His spiritual trajectory experienced an upturn in that challenging environment.

ASSIGNED TO PITTSBURGH

In 1961, with a bachelor's degree from Fairfield University in hand, Carpenter decided to join the staff of Young Life. So did his brother, Jack. There was only one staff opening locally and the Young Life area director in Pittsburgh needed help. Carpenter doesn't remember why, but he was chosen to go to Pittsburgh. He does remember that "Jack was happy and I was bitterly disappointed."

Bill Milliken, an early Young Life worker in New York (and subsequently founder of the national Communities in Schools organization that helps at-risk youth to succeed in school), joked that Young Life staff training back then was essentially "there's a high school, go get it." But from their interactions in New York and Milliken's occasional visits to Pittsburgh, he observed Carpenter's unusual effectiveness in youth leadership. "He had the gift of hanging out and the ability to relate to all types of people," Milliken said. "He was forthright in a caring way, very charismatic, with a sense of humor that could defuse tensions. I consider him one of the great practitioners of relational theology."

Carpenter started his Pittsburgh career with a visit to Wilkinsburg High School east of Pittsburgh. A popular senior greeted him at the door on behalf of the school's Young Life contingent; she would eventually become his wife. Reid also gained recognition by starting a Young Life group at the inner-city Northview Heights housing community. He was promoted to Pittsburgh area director in 1962.

As in New York, where Young Life's community work had generated threats from gangs, Pittsburgh's urban clientele was challenging. On bus trips to Young Life camp in Colorado, Milliken recalled, he had to ask participants to turn in their weapons before the trip started—and he sent one youth back home by Greyhound when he was caught violating the rule. According to Carpenter, when their bus was traveling through Indiana on a return trip from Colorado in 1964, white thugs fired shots at them.

Bold engagement with tough teens—and frustration with churches that seemed to prefer to steer clear of unchurched youth—helped to shape Carpenter's view of ministry, but an experience on Mount Washington shaped his commitment to Pittsburgh.

"I can remember Sam saying 'Boys, behold your city' to us," Carpenter said. "I remember thinking that my mission of winning a few high-school kids to Christ, as important as that was, needed to be connected to a broader vision that encompassed the whole city. I was overwhelmed but excited."

Groping to discern what to do with their inspiration, Carpenter and James made a covenant, committing themselves to each other and to Pittsburgh. (According to Carpenter, a permanent commitment seemed a bit intimidating, so they agreed to commit for 15 years and then reevaluate. James would live only eight more years.) Their interaction began with shared prayer times and grew into a substantial ministry partnership, as Carpenter joined with the Pittsburgh Experiment to launch its teen conferences at Oglebay beginning in 1964 and college conferences at Atwood Lake, Ohio in 1965. In 1967, Young Life–Pittsburgh moved into the Experiment's offices.

During Carpenter's early years as area director, Young Life–Pittsburgh teetered on the edge of financial collapse. One day he shared his desperation with James, who asked, "How much do you need?" Carpenter said he needed $3,000. "I think the Experiment has $3,000 in the bank. Why don't we just give it to you?" James replied. With his board's approval, this gift kept Young Life operating in Pittsburgh.

"Reid was like a family member," said Sue Zuk, James's daughter. "He was at the house a lot, and he named one of his sons after my father. He knew how to get teenagers' attention. He would do anything to get a laugh and then weave God into the story."

A KEY RECRUIT

Carpenter envisioned a pipeline for cultivating strong Christian leadership in Pittsburgh, from Young Life for high-schoolers to participation in the Pittsburgh Experiment for college graduates entering the business world. However, the weak link in the chain was the college years.

While speaking at a 1968 youth conference in Rhode Island, Carpenter felt "massively impressed" by the other speaker, John Guest—mainly because Guest traveled with a rock band. A British native, Guest had come to Christ at a Billy Graham crusade and had done youth ministry in the Philadelphia area. Music was a big part of his popularity at the time, especially since he looked and sounded like a Beatle.

Guest was equally impressed by Carpenter, whom he described as "an effective communicator—humorous, cool, a gifted evangelist. As I listened to him, I could perceive that he was worth getting to know."

Both men recalled, 50 years later, that an immediate bond developed between them that weekend. Guest's wife had worked for Young Life and had read some of Sam Shoemaker's books, so an invitation from Pittsburgh's Young Life leader to fulfill part of Shoemaker's vision for Pittsburgh resonated with him. Guest agreed to come to Pittsburgh in late 1968, initially as a Pittsburgh Experiment employee.

Guest noted that in 1968, hiring someone who came with a Christian rock band posed significant risk. "There were nationally recognized Christian leaders and institutions who said this kind of music was of the devil," he stated. "But I was not playing church—I was getting into secular situations where I could play and also talk about the Lord." He appreciated that both James and Carpenter were risk takers, although Guest and the band were still expected to support themselves. They did so by performing on college campuses and recording one of America's first contemporary Christian music albums.

Guest's arrival was a treat for teenage Sue Zuk, who would sneak down the steps to listen when he brought his guitar and Beatle-like looks to play for parties at James's home. When not strumming a guitar, however, Guest was more reserved, so it was quite a growing experience when he, James, Carpenter, and Paul Everett met for half a day of prayer and sharing. "They went around the room and talked about their struggles very vulnerably," Guest said. "Still very British and fresh off the boat, I wasn't ready to talk about stuff underneath my façade; it seemed very American to me. But gradually I learned to be real in relationships."

TAKING THE OFFENSIVE

Young Life exploded under Carpenter's leadership, from several hundred teens to several thousand—and not just in the inner city, but in wealthy suburbs like Mount Lebanon, Fox Chapel, and Churchill. This success and his association with the Pittsburgh Experiment brought Carpenter into contact with Christians who had disposable income. His biggest single funding source, however, came by coincidence.

Dora Hillman was the widow of J. Hartwell Hillman, whom a Pittsburgh newspaper called "the last of the city's great industrial tycoons." Hart Hillman made his fortune in the 1920s and died in 1959. Young Life worker Dale Craig met Dora Hillman at a retreat in 1967, and she invited him to write to her if he needed support. When a $3,000 check from Dora Hillman showed up at the Young Life office, Carpenter immediately recognized the name and made an appointment with her. Hillman would soon become a strategic contributor to the burgeoning network of evangelical leaders in Pittsburgh.

Carpenter and James's vision for the city caused them to ask other Christian leaders to begin convening on a monthly basis. With James's death in 1969, Guest became Carpenter's main partner in launching the group, named the Pittsburgh Offensive to stress its concern for making an impact on Pittsburgh, not just having fellowship. Initially, Hillman hosted the meetings at her residence in the Laurel Highlands east of Pittsburgh.

Offensive meetings never had a formal action agenda, but they followed a prescribed pattern. After introductions, initial prayer, and singing, Carpenter—who missed only a couple Offensive meetings in 20 years—would reiterate their reason for being together: "We are here to pray that Pittsburgh will become known for Jesus Christ." Someone would lead a Bible study, and then most of the time was spent taking prayer requests and hearing whatever people wanted to share about their life and ministry, or "reports from the front lines." After an extended period of prayer, the group would share a meal together.

One might have expected the Offensive to quickly become oversubscribed due to the chance to rub shoulders with influential Christian leaders, but it operated by word of mouth and with no publicity. "The only criterion for participation was showing up," Carpenter said. "We found that those who did not feel called to a citywide vision simply weeded themselves out."

Most of the early participants were parachurch leaders like Paul Everett, Jim Leckie of Youth Guidance, and Bob Letsinger of the Pittsburgh Power and Light Company, a college-age outreach housed at First Presbyterian Church downtown. To balance the parachurch emphasis, the Offensive added pastors such as Bob Lamont of First Presbyterian, Dick Todd of Memorial Park Presbyterian, and Tom Smith of Monumental Baptist in the Hill District. Mary Frances Irvin of Seton Hill University in Greensburg became one of the first Catholic voices.

The Offensive had no formal membership, but key participants were expected to attend regularly. People who said they would have to miss a meeting could expect Carpenter to ask, "What do you have that's more important than this?"

Carpenter described the Offensive's theory of change as linking ideas, power, and authority. Typically, he explained, people with ideas must secure permission to implement them from people with authority, whom they cannot access directly, so they need someone with power to bring the authority figure to the table. In the Offensive's case, most of the participants were idea people; Dora Hillman exerted the power that could attract authority figures by offering her sumptuous residence as a meeting location. "When you invited people to come to Dora Hillman's house overnight, you rarely got a no," Carpenter observed. "That atmosphere made people believe that they were doing something important together."

The network also built connections to other powerful Pittsburgh-area Christian leaders, such as Alcoa executive Fred Fetterolf. Thus, for example, when idea people (like Young Life leaders seeking to reach troubled youth) wanted to get the attention of someone in authority (like a school superintendent), they enlisted people like Fetterolf to make the call.

MEMORABLE SPINOFFS

The early years of the Offensive generated several long-lasting projects, beginning with the Ligonier Valley Study Center. Dora Hillman had a high opinion of R. C. Sproul, a Pittsburgh native who had studied under the great Reformed apologist John Gerstner at Pittsburgh Theological Seminary and then became associate pastor at College Hill Presbyterian Church in Cincinnati. (Sproul's boss at College Hill, Jerry Kirk, had led an enormously successful Young Life group at Mount Lebanon United Presbyterian Church in suburban Pittsburgh before going to Cincinnati.) Guest was a fan of Sproul too, having heard him in Philadelphia, where Sproul taught at the Conwell School of Theology before it merged into Gordon-Conwell Seminary in 1969. Sproul had also spoken at one of the Pittsburgh Experiment's college retreats at Atwood Lake, Ohio.

Hillman persuaded Sproul to come to the Laurel Highlands and become the resident teacher and theologian at a study center modeled after Francis Schaeffer's L'Abri community in Switzerland. He lived up to expectations, presenting Bible studies to packed crowds in the summer while he and his staff also hosted seminars and retreats for numerous church groups and other organizations. Moreover, the Ligonier Valley Study Center developed a robust audio and video ministry that made Sproul a highly sought-after speaker. In 1984, he relocated his ministry to Orlando, Florida, which became his home base for his last 33 years.

Also in 1970, James and Carpenter's vision of a regional college ministry took wings. John Guest had become a part-time youth pastor at St. Stephen's Episcopal Church in Sewickley while continuing to perform with the Excursions in college settings. Guest wanted to develop a mechanism to follow up with young people who expressed spiritual interest at the concerts, but his work was already dwarfing the Pittsburgh Experiment's primary focus on the business world; officially, the Experiment's staff at this point consisted of Everett, a secretary, and four band members!

Discouraged at his inability to expand the college outreach and clashing somewhat in style with the more sedate Everett, Guest was pursuing an Episcopal church pastorate in Michigan when conversations with Carpenter and others resulted in St. Stephen's giving him $10,000 to start a new organization, the Coalition for Christian Outreach. Departing from the traditional model of campus ministry used by independent parachurch groups like InterVarsity and Campus Crusade, the Coalition envisioned having local congregations sponsor staff who would serve both the church and a nearby college campus. By 1974, it had staff working on 27 campuses in Pennsylvania, Ohio, and West Virginia.

Guest served as executive director for only one year before becoming senior pastor at St. Stephen's, but his replacement, Bob Long, stayed for 38 years as executive and then as chairman. The Coalition has held Jubilee, one of the nation's largest Christian student conferences, in Pittsburgh since 1977. Today it is considered one of the most effective campus ministry organizations in helping Christian students understand how to approach their studies, construct a consistent worldview, and impact their culture.

The Offensive also spawned another ambitious spinoff of lasting importance. After he became rector of St. Stephen's Episcopal Church in 1971 (with a contract that gave him two weeks off each year for rock-and-roll festivals), he initiated a discussion within the Offensive about starting a ministry training program in conjunction with the British theological college where he had studied. R. C. Sproul instead challenged him to start an evangelical-leaning seminary in the Pittsburgh area. In 1975, Trinity Episcopal School for Ministry opened with 17 students; it has since grown into a widely recognized evangelical training center with influence far beyond the North American Episcopal/Anglican context (see chapter 8).

THE LEADER IS SET FREE

The single biggest Offensive spinoff, however, was the one that took its leader along for a 25-year ride.

By 1978, Carpenter was chafing against what he saw as the restrictions, demands, and aloofness of Young Life's national leadership. He objected to what he considered its increasingly bureaucratic nature, relative inattention to urban problems, and lack of racial diversity. He was also drawn to addressing the social needs of which he became acutely aware through Pittsburgh Offensive discussions. After 17 years with Young Life, he was ready to leave but had nowhere obvious to go.

The turning point came when Carpenter was presenting a report on needs and opportunities in Pittsburgh. "Everything was getting handed off to someone who was already busy, so it was a time of frustration," Carpenter said. "Everyone knew we were coming up against a wall."

Jim Leckie of Youth Guidance stood up and said, "Reid, you have to leave Young Life and lead this full-time. Do we all agree?" Those present agreed, in effect commissioning Carpenter to form a new organization.

In August 1978, Carpenter resigned from Young Life and became president of the Pittsburgh Leadership Foundation. He placed the word *Foundation* in the title to communicate a sense of substance and prominence, even though, unlike most foundations, the PLF would have to raise money before it could spend any. Dora Hillman wrote a $250,000 check to launch the organization. The initial board had other people of influence too, such as community college president John Hirt, R. K. Mellon Foundation officer Larry Surdoval, lawyer Frank Wiegand, and Nanky Chalfant, wife of a Sewickley businessman and member of Guest's church who would become the host of Offensive meetings after Hillman died in 1982. Chalfant personally gave over $1 million to the PLF.

FIRST TARGET: ADDICTION

Quite appropriately, since Carpenter traced his commitment to Pittsburgh back to his encounter with Sam Shoemaker—the clergyman who inspired Alcoholics Anonymous—the PLF's first project was in the addiction field.

By the 1970s, drugs were a scourge in high schools across the United

States, greatly impacting Carpenter's personal life not only as a Young Life area leader but as a father of four children. "We asked what Pittsburgh was doing to protect its children from this overwhelming reality," he explained. "I didn't have an answer, but now I had a foundation."

Carpenter also had a knack for uniting people in coalitions. Drawing on a general familiarity with recovery spirituality that dated back to his exposure to Sam Shoemaker, he and the PLF called all the region's major organizations involved in drug and alcohol services to come together, and they became partners in founding the Coalition for Addictive Diseases (COAD).

COAD helped to make Pittsburgh an attractive candidate for federal research grants on addiction because everyone in the city was collaborating rather than competing. In 1979, with COAD's support, an inpatient adolescent drug and alcohol treatment center opened at the city's St. Francis Hospital.

As he did throughout his career, Carpenter creatively seized the opportunity to endear himself to key leaders and leverage those relationships for creative ministry. In one case, he took a teenage girl to St. Francis for drug treatment and subsequently discovered that her father, a top executive at a major Pittsburgh corporation, was struggling with alcohol abuse. Carpenter offered personal support for the executive's recovery; later, he requested and received permission for COAD to hold meetings in that corporation's boardroom. "The people who work in that field don't get much respect," he explained. "When they felt a genuine embrace from a corporate executive's largesse, it appealed to their basic need to be respected and treated with dignity."

Karen Plavan, a treatment consultant who attended her first COAD meeting in 1982 and subsequently became a COAD volunteer and then a PLF consultant, agreed with Carpenter's assessment: "Reid wanted to lift up the people who worked in the addiction treatment field. Having the president of a large corporation host them for lunch meetings sounds like something small, but it helped COAD members feel valued and important, especially since their lifesaving work generally received little compensation or recognition."

Carpenter brought another powerful leader into the loop when Fran Fetterolf, wife of Alcoa executive Fred Fetterolf, became COAD's first coordinator. Carpenter himself remained the organization's executive committee chair for 20 years. In the early 1990s, at Plavan's encouragement, COAD became CLEAR (Coalition on Leadership, Education and Advocacy for Recovery) to emphasize a more positive focus on recovery rather than on the problem itself.

Still operating under Plavan's leadership, CLEAR at age 40 claims to be the oldest substance abuse coalition in America. Among its major achievements, Plavan cited a Robert Wood Johnson Foundation "demand treatment" grant to address the common problem of people's inability to access addiction treatment at the point of need; a pilot program to screen emergency room patients for possible alcohol or drug problems; CLEAR's launching of the Pittsburgh Pastoral Care Conference, now 18 years old; and improved partnering with the county jail to address drug and alcohol issues among offenders. To Plavan, all those successes flowed out of Carpenter's initial ability to facilitate cooperation among players who would normally have been competing against each other for clients and grant money.

COAD even found open doors in Russia after Luis Dolan, a Catholic priest active in Soviet-American partnerships to battle alcoholism, asked Pittsburgh addictions counselor Terry Webb to host a delegation from the Russian Orthodox Church seeking to learn about effective community-based prevention programs. Webb immediately turned to COAD, which initiated its Russian Project. From 1992 to 2002, COAD members planted prevention and recovery programs in Russia and provided training to Russian physicians. When other former Communist countries requested help, the Russian Project changed its name to Global Outreach for Addiction Leadership and Learning (GOAL) and became a separate nonprofit entity that continues to operate today, based in Lancaster, Pennsylvania.

COLLABORATING WITH ALL PEOPLE OF GOOD WILL

COAD flourished because a Christian organization brought a cross-section of key players into collaboration. That doesn't happen often, for two reasons: non-Christians don't want to work under Christian auspices, and Christians don't want to dilute their spiritual message by having unbelievers in their organizations.

The PLF's approach to working hand in hand with all people of good will, demonstrated in COAD's founding and many times thereafter, reflects Carpenter's own evolution from Young Life evangelism to a model of "kingdom entrepreneurship." Carpenter approached the issue in terms of concentric circles. On matters of Christian evangelism, he pointed out, only Christians can be partners; on social issues like those addressed in Matthew 25:35–36 (caring for the poor, strangers, the sick, or prisoners), the circle is larger because anyone who shares those concerns can be a colleague.

Carpenter contended further, however, that Christians need to move beyond their own community to be effective. "Our own stages are so small," he said of most Christian organizations. "At the PLF, we were good at getting people on the same stage with us who didn't necessarily believe all the same things as us. If you get to know me, you are going to get to know Jesus. Similarly, if you attended a Labor-Management Prayer Breakfast [an early PLF project described in chapter 6], you wouldn't hear an altar call, but you would hear that Jesus Christ is our basis for reconciliation."

Plavan again backed up Carpenter's claims, based on her COAD/CLEAR experience: "Reid was a great example of how a Christian can respect and work with people of all faiths. If he said 'Lord Jesus' when praying for someone, nobody got upset, even though we had Jewish and Muslim participation."

That cooperation included broad ecumenism as well. "Making Pittsburgh famous for God required ecumenism," Carpenter said. "You cannot do this without the whole church taking the whole gospel to the whole city." To sustain ecumenical unity, Carpenter focused on Scripture, prayer, singing, and personal testimony while avoiding debates over disputed points of theology. The only significant dissenter from this worldview within the Offensive/PLF orbit was Sproul, whose firmly Reformed theological framework limited his ability to partner with Catholics.

The Offensive's original Catholic participant, Sister Mary Francis Irvin, arranged unusually robust prayer support for the PLF. In 1985, having retired from her position at Seton Hill University, Irvin recruited seven groups of nuns to pray daily for the PLF's projects, participating churches, and ministries represented in the Offensive (which continued to meet monthly through 1990). "A log was kept of all the requests and how God answered," said Mary Beth Gasior, then the PLF prayer coordinator. "The sisters loved hearing the results of their prayers."

The big advantage of the PLF's broadly cooperative spirit was that it attracted funds from sources not generally associated with Christian giving. Westinghouse supported PLF in bringing Milliken's Communities in Schools organization (originally called Cities in Schools) to Pittsburgh. Alcoa invested heavily in Garfield Jubilee, a housing and neighborhood improvement project in the city's Garfield community.

MAKING PEOPLE WANT TO GIVE

Frequently, the pathway to corporate support went through individual Christians who worked at those companies. For many years, Carpenter led a Bible study attended by prominent business leaders like Fetterolf of Alcoa, Bill Roemer of Integra Bank, Jay Roy of the Federal Home Loan Bank, Carl Grefenstette of the Hillman Company, Jim Gregory of Calgon Carbon, Jack Hoy of Peoples Gas, and Tom Smith of Ketchum Public Relations. Also on his list of close contacts were Tom Murrin of Westinghouse, Tom Usher of U.S. Steel, and the Donahue family of Federated Investors.

That impressive list of contacts raises a question: how did Carpenter, not himself a person of wealth, relate to the rich and powerful and persuade them to give generously to the causes he espoused?

Carpenter presented a simple theory of fundraising: it's all based on relationships. He summarized his approach to people of wealth as follows: "I would count it a treasure to be your friend. I will listen to you, be available to you, and never back off if you have a need. Conversely, being my friend means you won't refuse to talk to me about money. You can't carry your money to heaven—it's too heavy. I have to talk to you about money because I represent a lot of people who are trying to serve the needy, and guess what you have that they need? I will never push you to give me money, but I will always let you know about the need. You have money, God wants it, and I will help you give it if that's what you want."

Plavan, who observed Carpenter's interactions for many years, highlighted his concern for people's inner lives, not just their professional lives. "In our culture, we tend to separate personal life from work life," she stated. "But if Reid had a relationship with you, he cared about your life and family. He took the time to say, 'Tell me about yourself.'"

AN IMPRESSIVE INTERMEDIARY

When young medical doctor David Hall wanted to start a healthcare ministry for the underserved in Pittsburgh, the PLF made it happen. Carpenter connected Hall with pastor Doug Dunderdale of Eastminster Presbyterian Church, who had the same burden on his own heart. Eastminster provided the space, the PLF funded an administrator for the first six months, and the East Liberty Family Health Care Center opened as an exemplary source of "whole-person" healthcare in 1982.

Thirty-six years later, the center receives over 30,000 patient visits a year at four locations, the tireless Dr. Hall is still its medical director, and the PLF still receives credit for launching one of the most respected faith-based operations in Pittsburgh.

This was one of the PLF's easiest spinoffs, as the health center became an independent organization within a year of the initial investment. But it typifies the genius of the PLF's intermediary function. Carpenter stumbled into this role more by practice than by theory as he aligned a citywide vision, an assessment of priority needs, and a set of relationships with donors who trusted him.

Since then, others have developed more rigorous arguments for the value of an intermediary, which David Hillis describes in *Cities: Playgrounds or Battlegrounds?* as "any organization whose sole purpose of existence is to facilitate collaboration to ensure that all the disparate parts of a city can function in healthy, effective, and empowered ways."

Thanks to the PLF, people concerned for Pittsburgh's welfare came together as collaborators rather than trying to work separately. Hillis argues that this model leads to clearer focus on how to address the city's challenges, relationships that provide mutual encouragement, better mobilization of resources, better coordination and understanding of roles, and skill development.

In Hillis's view, city-level leadership foundations have three main functions: connecting leaders, building capacity, and taking joint action. To fulfill these three functions, a leadership foundation should (1) have a strategy for engaging the whole city, (2) work with people of good faith and goodwill, (3) mobilize the resources of the church at large, (4) have a plan to make resources available for capacity building, (5) have an effective executive and management team, (6) secure solid financing, (7) be able to tell its story, and (8) have evaluation metrics in place to measure impact.

Hillis formerly headed the Northwest Leadership Foundation in Tacoma, Washington and is currently president of Leadership Foundations, an umbrella entity that oversees and supports similar organizations as far away as South Africa and India. And yes, that worldwide replication all started in Pittsburgh.

AN UNPLANNED REPLICATION

"There was never a plan or decision to replicate," Carpenter insisted. But there was a natural target audience: his Young Life friends. Carpenter had peers across the United States who loved their cities but couldn't work effectively with kids any longer because they had become "Old Life." When they visited Carpenter in Pittsburgh, he would take them to visit PLF projects. By the mid-1980s, some of them were asking Carpenter to visit their cities, meet with local leaders, and help them create similar organizations.

The first replication happened in Chicago, followed by Philadelphia, Memphis, Knoxville, Tacoma, and others. By 1993 there were a dozen leadership foundations, whose leaders met quarterly on an informal basis to share ideas, encourage each other, and laugh together. At that point, sensing a need for more extensive, experienced guidance, the group of founders asked the PLF board if they could buy a portion of Carpenter's time. The PLF agreed, and Carpenter became president of the Council of Leadership Foundations (now called simply Leadership Foundations).

Since starting similar organizations elsewhere was not in Carpenter's original vision, this part of the story is better told from below—that is, by some of the recipients of the PLF's wisdom, leadership foundation developers Larry Lloyd (Memphis, founded in 1987), Chris Martin (Knoxville, 1994), and David Hillis (Tacoma, 1994).

Reid Carpenter addresses his peers at a Leadership Foundations meeting in Seattle. Urban ministry expert Ray Bakke is behind him.

Initially, replication largely consisted of learning from the PLF's experience and being magnetized to Carpenter's stories and personality. "If he met someone who thought the way he did, he'd invite you to consider joining the leadership foundation movement overnight," Lloyd joked.

"In many such organizations, you go in for training as if you've developing a franchise," Martin stated. "There was none of that here—just themes and principles, a theology of place, a commitment to the church, and a real vision for mobilizing the laity." Martin stressed the impact of devotion to a particular place, noting that "if something didn't work, I couldn't move away. I had to try again or figure out a different way to attack that particular need."

Hillis agreed that initially, more knowledge was caught than taught: "There was no systematic concretization of how leadership foundations worked. It was inspiration to love your city, and then Reid would tell story after story." But he suggested that particular instincts were consistently replicated, such as a citywide vision, connecting the boardroom with the street, ecumenism, the power of relationships, the relevance of recovery spirituality, and the adhesiveness of humor.

For Martin, the process of starting a leadership foundation mainly involved hearing stories from other cities and then "having God percolate in your minds how to contextualize it for your own city." When Martin first called Carpenter to talk about starting a foundation and said he had experience with Young Life, Carpenter replied, "That's the first thing you have to have." Later in the conversation, Martin mentioned having been fired from a neighborhood organization over an internal dispute. "That's the second thing," Carpenter laughed. "You have to have been fired from somewhere."

Hillis commented that Carpenter and John Hirt, the retired community college president who would develop the Leadership Foundations accreditation system, combined "an attractive way to think about the city" with a humble recognition that the specific methods and programs would have to differ across cities. "It was always clear," he said, "that we were about not a product but a process—engaging people of good will for city initiatives."

"We almost carbon-copied everything" from the PLF, Lloyd said, but over time Memphis generated innovative new applications. For example, the Memphis foundation provides back-office support for both its own spinoffs and other nonprofits.

To Lloyd, one key to leadership foundations' success is their willingness to take a back seat, never claiming that the programs they support are "our" programs. "People come to us because they see us as a servant organization that wants the city to prosper, not a top-down leader," he explained.

As the movement grew, so did a recognition of the need for quality control. The need became acute in the early 1990s when an organization sought funding from the Lilly Endowment (which had long been involved in the network's development) calling itself a leadership foundation but none of the "real" leadership foundations knew who this organization was.

In Hillis's view, Hirt created the leadership foundation accreditation process "out of his recognition that if the Leadership Foundations movement was to grow, it would need discipline and rigor. John felt that borrowing the accreditation process from higher education gave us the best chance to do that."

The initial round of accreditation involved Carpenter and Hirt visiting a leadership foundation for three days and investigating four questions: (1) Who do you say you are? (2) How are you demonstrating that? (3) What is the impact or outcome? (4) How are you providing resources for the work? Over the years, the review process has become less onerous, relying more on data and interviews and requiring less preparation of written narratives.

Hillis acknowledged that soaking up Carpenter's experiences could be daunting at times: "He'd say you need to get to know your business community and be on a first-name basis with organized labor too, and we'd all walk out feeling no one else could do what Reid has done." But Hillis believes that, by isolating the core functions that make leadership foundations work, the network of organizations has captured the PLF's DNA and replicated it fruitfully, from Dallas to Delhi.

As the man who took over network leadership from Carpenter, Hillis especially praised the graciousness with which he implemented the handover while remaining accessible as a resource. "Many successions in Christian settings are train wrecks," Hillis contended; "the founder maintains hold on all the levers of power and the next person does not survive." He described Carpenter as having learned from those before him, like Sam Shoemaker, Dora Hillman, Fred Fetterolf, and Nanky Chalfant—all "remarkable people with power who held onto it loosely."

Hillis, Lloyd, and Martin all treasured the depth, openness, and hilarity of the leaders' retreats. "That drew me into a family," Martin said. "I felt that I was walking with brothers who really cared about me." They also observed that Carpenter's connections—and his willingness to share them with others—paid enormous dividends when the George W. Bush administration opened up new funding opportunities for faith-based organizations in 2002. Many leadership foundations, for example, received federal funding to serve children of incarcerated parents through their Amachi programs, modeled on the one created in Philadelphia by former mayor Wilson Goode (himself a backer of the Philadelphia Leadership Foundation).

Dave Hillis (right) presents Reid Carpenter with a plaque in 2008 as he succeeds Carpenter as president of the Leadership Foundations organization.

Ironically, the mother of all leadership foundations no longer follows what has become a worldwide pattern. After Carpenter gave up the PLF's reins, his successor, John Stahl-Wert, began to shift the organization toward a primary focus on leadership development rather than on conceiving, incubating, and implementing community projects. The PLF today continues to be a valuable force in Pittsburgh, but it is very different from the PLF of 1978 to 2003.

A PLF fundraising booklet prepared in 2003 claimed that over 25 years, the PLF had raised $86 million and generated $494 million in value. That last figure was heavily skewed by the PLF's role in developing the World Vision International Distribution Center, which had distributed donated items worth $350 million. Even if one leaves out that significant instance of global resource distribution, however, it was quite a 25-year run.

A PITTSBURGHER BASED IN FLORIDA

In 2004, a year after resigning as PLF president, Reid Carpenter, at age 66, moved to Florida. That typical southward swing by a senior would be unremarkable except for one thing: Carpenter had committed his life to Pittsburgh and then, 42 years later, he left.

Carpenter moved mainly to support his wife Carole's new career opportunity. Carole had worked in administration at Franciscan University of Steubenville, Ohio. When her boss there left Franciscan to help Domino's Pizza founder Tom Monaghan create a new conservative Catholic university—and a whole new town—20 miles inland from Naples, Florida, Carole became part of the development team. Ave Maria University opened at a temporary site in Naples in 2003 and moved into its stunning permanent campus in 2007.

While at Franciscan, the American university most closely affiliated with the Catholic charismatic movement, Carole was so struck by the vibrant spirituality of the students around her that she started attending chapel services there and experienced a powerful sense of personal renewal. Her experience initiated a new chapter in Reid's spiritual journey as well.

Carole and Reid Carpenter near Vail, Colorado, where they travel frequently for fellowship and accountability retreats with colleagues dating back to their Young Life days.

"One day, she asked me if I would mind if she became Catholic," Reid said. "I started going to mass with her. The music was terrible, but I could not believe the awe I saw in normal people when they went up to receive the Eucharist."

Ruth Malos, Carpenter's personal secretary, recalled the day when her boss asked her to make three appointments with Bishop Donald Wuerl of Pittsburgh's Catholic Diocese. She didn't know why at the time, but those were the first of seven monthly meetings at which Bishop Wuerl personally catechized the PLF president toward the Catholic Church.

As Reid contemplated this step, Catholic teaching on the real presence of Christ in communion remained an obstacle to him. Before his last meeting with Bishop Wuerl, he contacted well-known Catholic apologist Scott Hahn, who had become a Christian through Carpenter's Young Life ministry in the early 1970s, served as a Presbyterian pastor, but then converted to Catholicism and has taught at Franciscan University since 1990.

"You taught me all about the real presence of Jesus Christ," Hahn said. Carpenter was quite confused, but Hahn continued: "You were the speaker on a Young Life retreat and told us all about Jesus Christ. You then invited us to go outside and say a prayer of faith, and Jesus himself would come into our hearts. And so I did … and he did. That's how I first believed Jesus makes his presence very real within my heart. I took him at his word.

"So when I heard him say in John 6 that whoever eats his flesh and drinks his blood *abides* in me, once again I took him at his word, just as all believers in the church did for the first 1,500 years. If Jesus can make his presence so real to us within our hearts, no wonder he wants to continue feeding us with himself, really and truly."

By the time Carpenter got to Bishop Wuerl's office, he no longer needed to be convinced.

When we visited Reid Carpenter in January 2018, he and Carole had been enjoying their lives together in Florida for 14 years. But he never got out of the leadership foundation business. In addition to leading and then consulting the international network of leadership foundations, he started one in Immokalee, an impoverished, migrant-dominated community northeast of Naples.

He also never fully got out of Pittsburgh. On the contrary, the biggest spiritually driven event to occur in Pittsburgh during 2017 was conceived by Reid Carpenter. The initial groundwork for that event was laid in late 2016, when he persuaded Bishop David Zubik to invite local evangelical leaders to a series of five prayer and worship sessions. "Even most evangelicals tend to respond when they get a letter from the bishop," Carpenter quipped.

Zubik had known Carpenter since his time as Bishop Wuerl's secretary, before going to Green Bay, Wisconsin as bishop and then returning to lead the Pittsburgh Diocese upon Wuerl's promotion to cardinal. He described his confidence in Carpenter as "instantaneous. He is as real as you can get, had lots of connections, and used them in ways that honor the Lord."

The group met five times, worshiping in a range of styles from black gospel to contemplative Taizé. In May 2017, as the last session approached and members wondered what should grow out of this sharing time, Carpenter gave Zubik another idea: propose a joint event the day after Thanksgiving at which members of Pittsburgh congregations would pack a million boxed meals for the needy.

Zubik thought the logistics were unachievable; Carpenter demonstrated otherwise. He brought in the Naples-based Meals of Hope organization, which specializes in coordinating food packing events. He also secured funds to cover the food costs and rent the Pittsburgh Convention Center for the event, called Amen to Action. On November 24, three thousand Pittsburgh-area Christians came downtown to worship together and then were deployed on assembly lines. According to the official count, they exceeded their goal by preparing 1,014,366 meals for distribution through southwestern Pennsylvania's food bank network.

TOWARD GREAT STEWARDSHIP

After telling one of his more vexing parables, in Luke 16, Jesus suggested that the "people of the light" (his followers) were less shrewd about using earthly wealth than the "people of this world." In modern times, that dictum often seems to be confirmed. Government, educational institutions, and businesses seem to prize coordination and efficiency, but God's people are divided into many separate groups. In contrast, the Pittsburgh Offensive and the Pittsburgh Leadership Foundation demonstrated the enormous benefit of expanding the vision of believers within a metropolitan area and bringing them together to imagine and implement things that could happen only through regionwide collaboration.

Sustaining that collaboration is difficult, due to busy schedules, conflicting theological convictions, and parochial interests. Even the PLF discovered that after it launched a project called Pittsburgh 2000 to harness and exploit the broad cooperation that had surrounded Billy Graham's 1993 crusade in the city. When the organization tried to translate that unity into practical action in a specific community, turf battles between individual congregations deflated the energy.

But over and over, the PLF brought a wide range of leaders together to make a lasting impact. One reason was its ability to do what Sam Shoemaker did for Reid Carpenter in 1962—to rivet his attention on the whole city as his parish. Another reason was money. Carpenter had a knack for helping wealthy believers to see that their money was too heavy to carry to heaven and to inspire them to invest generously in Christian work. In that regard, Bill Gates, though his commitment is to secular philanthropy, seems more perceptive than most of the body of Christ.

Along with failing to give generously, Christians often forget to laugh. Perhaps awareness of the depth of human need makes them more somber, or perhaps they overreact to the raunchy nature of so much of what the world calls comedy. If so, they should learn from this chapter. Reid Carpenter and Young Life attracted youth to Christ through humor, he used humor to draw people to planning meetings, and he and his leadership foundation colleagues relied on humor to stay energized for years of inner-city work.

Finally, the PLF powerfully embodies the common adage that you can get a lot done if you don't care who gets the credit. Its funders and the projects it supported knew the PLF's significance, but to the general public it was invisible. It appears to have been featured in Pittsburgh newspapers just once between 1984 and 2003, when, on the organization's 25th anniversary, the *Pittsburgh Post-Gazette* credited it with creating or nurturing 40 local ministries and spawning 40 similar foundations across the country. That is a truly stunning level of under-the-radar accomplishment, and a reminder that great networking does not require a high public profile.

Six

A HOLE IN HIS HEAD, GOD'S LOVE FOR ALL IN HIS HEART:
WAYNE ALDERSON AND VALUE OF THE PERSON

Visitors touring the American Steel Foundry plant of Amsted Rail in Granite City, Illinois (near St. Louis) are typically surprised by what they see. Throughout the facility—which is unusually clean for a foundry—employees wave, give thumbs-up signs, and offer to talk about what they do. It feels more like a community than a workplace. Of course, no group of 800 workers is unanimously happy, as employees' online reviews indicate, but many describe caring supervisors and even a family environment.

Every department at American Steel has "point men," or people who stay abreast of employees' concerns and raise them with management at regular meetings. And if you come on the right day, you might find 20 employees gathered for a lunchtime Bible study, which plant managers sometimes attend.

"A lot of employees tell us their home lives are better," said Paul

Limbach, Amsted Rail's chief operating officer. "It's not a storybook place, but it's definitely different."

When visitors ask for an explanation of how American Steel became this way, Limbach gives them a copy of a nearly 40-year-old book called *Stronger Than Steel*. That's because the positive culture at American Steel is a direct, living legacy of the book's protagonist, Wayne Alderson, who led an even more stunning transformation of a similar plant near Pittsburgh in 1973.

Stronger Than Steel, one of the first books by famed Reformed author and theologian R. C. Sproul, vividly chronicled the amazing life of Wayne Alderson up to its publication in 1980. But there's a lot more to say about Alderson, who died in 2013, and his Value of the Person organization, which continues (under his daughter's leadership) to assist businesses across North America in meaningfully implementing love, dignity, and respect in the workplace.

AN UNFORGETTABLE SACRIFICE

Wayne Alderson was born in 1926, the fourth child of a fourth-generation coal miner in Canonsburg, southwest of Pittsburgh. At that time, their section of Canonsburg was a company town. The Aldersons lived in mining company housing and shopped at the company store, which meant that their debts to the company often exceeded Lank Alderson's wages.

The miners, trapped in a life of long, dangerous work for low pay, were seeking to unionize, and the company was determined to break up the union. As a result, young Wayne gained a deep appreciation of labor-management conflict in a setting where, in Sproul's words, "a miner's status was often measured by the number and size of the scars on his head left by the police."

Lank Alderson wanted his sons to become miners, but he harbored no illusions about whether his company appreciated him. Often, after an exhausting workday, he would tell his wife, "Edith, if they'd only value me as much as they value the mule." As Wayne explained many years later, that comment was no exaggeration:

In those days, mine mules were well trained and well kept. They were the high tech of the mines since they were the best advance warning system a mine had against explosions. It was a known fact that the mine owners considered it much easier and cheaper to replace a miner than to replace a well-trained mule. My father's desire to be treated as well as a mule left an indelible mark on me.

When Lank Anderson broke his leg in an on-the-job fall, his spirit was broken too. Unable to work, he was evicted from company housing and abandoned the family. Penniless, Wayne's mother gave her youngest child to relatives and set up a tent on a vacant Canonsburg lot, where she and her other six children lived for several months. "I remember looking out the tent flaps with my brothers and sisters and seeing houses on the hills of Canonsburg, aglow with electric lights," Wayne wrote later. "It looked like another world to us, a world of warmth and security that was beyond our grasp."

At age 18, Wayne Alderson volunteered for World War II. (He had tried to sneak into the military at age 15, but the recruiter knew his mother and turned him away.) Stationed in northeast France in February 1945, he volunteered to be one of his company's "point men," or advance scouts, along with his best friend Charles "Red" Preston. In that role, on March 15, 1945, he became the first American soldier to step into Germany. A few days later, after penetrating the heavily fortified Siegfried Line, he confronted a German soldier who threw a grenade at his feet. Wayne shot the soldier dead, but the grenade exploded and shattered his skull.

Semi-conscious and exposed to certain death, Wayne survived only because Red Preston wrapped his arms around him and shielded him. Red took a bullet in his head, laying down his life for his friend. Wayne survived, but with an indentation in his forehead. For the rest of his life, anyone who looked at Wayne would see an unmistakable scar, the reminder of his journey through the valley of death. His daughter Nancy Jean, as she grew up, would often hear him say, "I believe that God placed the hole in the middle of my forehead so that every day, when I woke up and looked in the mirror, I would be reminded that Red died for me."

Though spared by this living parable of Christ's sacrifice, Alderson would not experience his own spiritual awakening for another 20 years. As one of his admirers said of this time period, "He met his wife and they married, he went to college, he became an elder in the church [Pleasant Hills Community Presbyterian Church in suburban Pittsburgh], and then he became a Christian, and it was in that order."

One night in 1965, Alderson awoke from a dream with "Matthew 10:32" imprinted on his mind. He looked up the verse and read, "Whoever shall confess me before men, him will I confess also before my Father in heaven." At age 39, Alderson made that confession.

THE MIRACLE OF PITTRON STEEL

In that same year, Alderson, by then equipped with a degree in accounting and business administration, joined the financial department of Pittron Steel in Glassport, 12 miles southeast of Pittsburgh. By 1969, he was Pittron's controller and chief financial officer. As such, he could see that the plant was struggling financially. Extreme labor strife was much of the problem.

In October 1972, Pittron's unionized employees walked off the job and stayed out for 84 days. During the wildcat strike, Sproul recounted, Alderson went on a retreat with some church friends at "a facility tucked away in a remote section of the mountains of western Pennsylvania." While there, Alderson was deeply touched as the retreat speaker challenged Christians "to put their faith and values to the test in the real world ... to come out from under the shelter of their steeples and into the marketplace." Sproul modestly omitted that the retreat site was the Ligonier Valley Study Center and that the speaker was R. C. Sproul.

Shortly thereafter, Alderson began interfacing with union leaders (even though he was not a member of the Pittron negotiating team) and achieved an end of the strike. As vice president of operations, he then initiated "Operation Turnaround," determined to eliminate labor-management bitterness as well. Alderson revolutionized the foundry's atmosphere by learning employees' names, walking the plant floor to interact with them, and personally thanking them at the end of their workday. On some days he extended his hours long enough to talk with workers from all three shifts. When his employees were dealing with illness or death in their family, Alderson showed up at the hospital or the funeral home. Drawing on his faith, his union upbringing, and his concern for reconciliation, he demonstrated that he valued every person at Pittron. As he did so, the changes were unmistakable—and not just during work hours. Employees' wives wrote Alderson notes of appreciation, explaining that their husbands were no longer coming home angry because they felt cared for at the workplace.

Soon the formerly fractious plant even had a weekly Bible study, although it was initially proposed by union president Sam Piccolo, not management. "I knew they were testing me," Alderson commented several years later. "After all, the ones who asked weren't even Christians." And in a July 1974 *Guideposts* magazine article, Alderson described himself as a reluctant preacher: "I knew sharing [God's] love, or witnessing,

Alderson shares with employees at the Pittron chapel.

was part of being a Christian, but I wasn't sure it was right for this situation. I certainly didn't want to use Christianity in the foundry." But by late May 1973, less than five months after the strike ended, a *Pittsburgh Post-Gazette* article titled "Religion Plays Role in Labor Relations at Glassport Firm" reported that 40 percent of Pittron's 430 employees were attending lunchtime Bible studies in a storage room converted into a chapel.

During the 1974 energy crisis, when low supplies and rationing actually made it hard for Americans to fill their gas tanks, Alderson convinced Pittron to let employees take whatever gas they needed from the company reserves, with no questions asked. When the gas ran out and Alderson didn't know what to do, a man who had heard about his gesture called and offered two thousand more gallons.

But that wasn't the biggest miracle. On November 9, 1973, while Alderson was discussing his emerging "value of the person" concept with U.S. Senator Robert Taft and industrial and political leaders in Canton, Ohio, a malfunction during the pouring of a 110,000-pound ladle of molten steel caused a huge fire, yet incredibly no one was injured. After the spilled hot metal had burned out, a worker pried open his charred locker to find everything burned or melted—except his paperback New Testament, which was barely singed.

It was called the "Miracle of Pittron," and it became famous in a powerful documentary by Robin Miller that would reach

Alderson and George Protz after the 1973 fire at Pittron Steel. The hard hat and shoes in Protz's locker were destroyed; the Bible survived.

the White House. After viewing the film, President Gerald Ford expressed his hope that Alderson's Value of the Person program could become a model for labor-management relations across America.

There was one more miracle: business results. Pittron went without a labor grievance for 21 months, during which productivity rose by 64 percent and sales quadrupled.

RELEASED TO A WIDER PULPIT

Starting in August 1973, "The Pittron Story," a four-page occasional company newsletter, delivered more spiritual inspiration than corporate details. The August issue featured the gift of a Bible from Piccolo, now a believer, to Alderson. "Truth has become the basis of a new relationship at Pittron," Piccolo said. "Our meetings [in the chapel] began with five or six people. Now after 13 weeks the program has reached hundreds of workers. ... The human relations element is now strongly present in our plant and the word 'brother' has gotten into the right perspective."

On January 20, 1974, the anniversary of the strike's end, a thousand people attended a "service of gratitude" to thank God for the changes at Pittron. In February 1974, both Pittsburgh newspapers featured Pittron's gift of free gas to its employees.

On March 31, with Easter approaching, Pittron president George Hager sent every employee a letter with a gift certificate for a canned ham at the nearby Orlando's supermarket. An accompanying letter from Alderson mentioned that John Yanderly of Pittron Department 14 had crafted metal castings of praying hands that would be "available at Orlando's when you call for the ham if you want one." For many years, the Glassport borough building was also graced by a set of Yanderly's praying hands.

Miller's documentary captured Pittron's transformation for wide distribution. Miller visited the plant out of personal interest (or perhaps with a potential film project in mind) and told Alderson after his tour, "You need to capture this. The world will never believe what I have seen." With Alderson's encouragement, Miller spent considerable time at the plant, mingling with workers, attending chapel sessions, and interviewing

Alderson and his two faithful co-presenters from the United Steelworkers, Lefty Scumaci (left) and Sam Piccolo (right).

union members and executives. He also filmed the first Value of the Person conference, a three-day event held in June 1974 to commemorate Pittron's 75th anniversary, with Westinghouse Electric Company CEO Don Burnham and Pennsylvania's lieutenant governor among the speakers. The only scene Miller had to reenact for his hour-long production was the fire.

In fact, Miller was on site to film the beginning of the end at Pittron. Textron, Pittron's parent company, capitalized on the foundry's smashing success to sell it to Milwaukee-based Bucyrus-Erie. Miller captured the scene in Pittron's chapel as alarmed workers asked Alderson if Pittron had been sold and stated ominously, "If we lose [Wayne], we'd have trouble here." Alderson spoke of the growing recognition their story was receiving and assured them, "If I leave, I'll take with me what you have given me. And I'd like to think I'm leaving a little of myself with each one of you."

The sale happened in October 1974. Alderson flew to Milwaukee three months later and spent a full day with Bucyrus-Erie's CEO, who said he could keep his job if he discontinued his innovative gestures of conviviality, like walking the floor with the workers and providing an office for the union president. Alderson declined. He returned home and told a Pittsburgh reporter, "We spent eight hours together, talking. I made a friend that day and lost my job."

"I was this close to saying yes, but I couldn't," Alderson said later when describing the interview. "[The CEO] was asking me not just to compromise, but to capitulate everything I stood for."

Alderson told Bucyrus-Erie that Pittron had four other good managers trained in his principles. All four were fired. By July 1976, the employees were on strike again; in 1981, the foundry closed permanently.

But for Alderson, the end of his job at Pittron was the beginning of a new career. As his wife, Nancy, told him, "You have been set free to take this message to the world." He was besieged by public speaking invitations and requests to mediate labor-management conflicts (which he frequently did for no pay), reportedly being shot at while trying to resolve a labor dispute in Tennessee.

In October 1975, *Miracle of Pittron* premiered at a Glassport school auditorium, with about 1,500 people in attendance. President Ford, who had previewed the film, sent his best wishes by telegram. (Never bashful about approaching the halls of power, Alderson had sent the President a five-page letter a year earlier, inviting him to visit Pittron.) Alderson's press release on the film premiere indicated that he had formed "an organization dedicated to improving the quality of work life in American industry."

Alderson's "organization" was pretty much himself. But two key partners added to his credibility: Piccolo, Pittron's union representative, and United Steelworkers international office staff member Francis "Lefty" Scumaci, who had visited Pittron to check out what was happening there and became a believer in both Alderson and Jesus Christ. Piccolo and Scumaci would be Alderson's union sidekicks at countless public appearances, corporate seminars, and prayer breakfasts over the next three decades.

The other key source of Alderson's credibility, of course, was demonstrated success. His ideas were not just theory—he had applied them at Pittron with amazing results.

A newspaper article on Alderson's October 1977 visit to Hamilton, Ontario—Canada's leading steel city—revealed his willingness to steal a line from Sam Shoemaker. It reported that Alderson told his audience, "My challenge is to make Hamilton as well known for God as for steel."

Presumably Alderson had gotten that line from Pittsburgh's master of networking for the kingdom of God, Reid Carpenter. The two met around that time after Carpenter was invited to a viewing of *Miracle of Pittron* and, in his typically edgy way, brought along a group of inner-city African Americans with Black Panther connections. The young men were in tears by the end of the film. Carpenter would become one of Alderson's biggest supporters and a presenter at numerous Value of the Person seminars.

Volkswagen, which had recently opened a plant an hour southeast of Pittsburgh, became one of Alderson's first major clients in 1978. By then, he had added a crucial resource that would greatly enhance his communication capacity: his daughter. Nancy Jean Alderson, upon graduating in communications from Grove City College, turned down other job offers out of a deep conviction that she was called to work for her dad. She never took another job. The professional relationship between father and daughter would endure for 35 years.

"My role was to help him create a seminar," Nancy Jean (now Nancy McDonnell) explained. The Value of the Person seminars that she developed would spread to corporations all over North America. The enterprise also upped its professionalism by relocating out of Alderson's basement to share office space with the fledgling Pittsburgh Leadership Foundation.

A BIG PRAYER BREAKFAST

Carpenter's organizing skill came in handy when Lefty Scumaci challenged Alderson to hold a major prayer breakfast that would highlight the need for labor and management to come together under God. With prominent support from Carpenter, John Guest of St. Stephen's Episcopal Church in Sewickley, and Robert Holland of Pittsburgh's fashionable

Shadyside Presbyterian Church, the first Labor-Management Prayer Breakfast took place on December 1–2, 1978. (Despite the title, it included Friday night seminars along with the Saturday morning breakfast at the Hilton Hotel in downtown Pittsburgh.)

National Steel Corporation CEO George Stinson (recruited by Guest, his pastor) and United Steelworkers president Lloyd McBride (with Stinson participating in the invitation) agreed to co-chair the event, making it a national news item. Pittsburgh Mayor Richard Caliguiri proclaimed Value of the Person Week. Pennsylvania Governor Dick Thornburgh, U.S. Senator John Heinz, and U.S. Secretary of Labor Ray Marshall were among the speakers.

The Labor-Management Prayer Breakfast became an annual Pittsburgh Leadership Foundation project and lasted for 13 years, with typical attendance of 2,000. The always-entertaining Tony Campolo, Baptist pastor and sociology professor at Eastern University near Philadelphia, was on the program each year, joined by prominent voices from business and labor. When the famous Solidarity movement—the first trade union movement behind the Iron Curtain—started in 1980, the prayer breakfast couldn't get Solidarity's leader, Lech Walesa, out of Poland, so it did the next best thing by flying in Walesa's stepfather, a New Jersey dock worker.

The prayer breakfasts were unmistakably ecumenical. Alderson and Carpenter were widely recognized evangelicals; Piccolo and Scumaci, Alderson's closest partners on the labor side, were Catholic. Pittsburgh Catholic Bishop Donald Wuerl consistently attended; Carpenter described Wuerl as a reconciling agent, thanks to his close relations with both business and labor, and "the most important validator of the Prayer Breakfast."

During those years Alderson was twice considered for U.S. Secretary of Labor (by Presidents Carter and Reagan) and even briefly contemplated a 1988 run for president. He also appeared on NBC's *Today* show in March 1985 to commemorate the 40th anniversary of his other claim to fame—his World War II penetration into Germany.

Alderson welcomes Stanislaw Walesa, stepfather of famed Polish union leader Lech Walesa, to the podium at a Labor-Management Prayer Breakfast.

A BOOK AS GOOD AS THE SEMINARS

Other than attending a Value of the Person seminar, the best way to grasp the uniqueness and power of Alderson's work is to read the careful formulation of his ideas in *Theory R Management*, coauthored with his daughter, Nancy Alderson McDonnell.

Alderson argued that all three prominent theories of business management—Theory X (employees need to be constantly monitored), Theory Y (employees should be supported and encouraged), and Theory Z (employees should be involved in decision making)—remain confrontational at their core. Even in Theories Y and Z, management still sets the rules; the driving force is "we say you must" rather than "let us" work together.

Theory R contains five fundamental concepts: doing what is *right*, building *relationships*, *reconciliation* as the fundamental goal, *responsibility* taken by everyone, and *results* as a by-product. Alderson emphasized that results must be the endpoint, not the beginning point; if building relationships becomes just a gimmick to improve business results, the effort will smack of insincerity and will not succeed. "Relationships are not engineered," he stated. "Those that are engineered usually turn out to be big disasters."

Theory R Management took what Alderson had done instinctively as a servant leader at Pittron and placed it in a management framework. For example, he used his bold decision to offer his employees free gasoline during the 1973 energy crisis as an illustration of a virtually ubiquitous systemic problem in corporate America: the presence of "palace guards" who intervene between top executives and rank-and-file employees. In his determination to show Pittron employees that he personally cared about them, Alderson explained, "I refused to be intimidated by my palace guards" who thought that giving away a precious commodity would set a horrible precedent. Similarly, when describing his efforts to address deplorable work conditions at Pittron, Alderson drew a contrast between his belief that basic conditions should never be a matter of negotiation and the palace guards' view that management should never do anything for the union without extracting concessions in exchange.

The book puts meat on the Value of the Person mantra of "love, dignity, and respect" with numerous specifics, such as listening to people without a preconceived agenda, showing concern for every aspect of people's lives and not just their work productivity, being present in times of crisis, writing notes of appreciation, and offering practical assistance to victims of layoffs. It also gives examples of actions that can subtly show disrespect, like not telling employees what was done with their suggestions or giving a higher-quality bonus party to managers than to other workers.

Theory R Management is interpersonally sensitive but not spineless.

It offers guidance on isolating and neutralizing managers who refuse to value the people they manage, and on gearing policies toward the 90 percent of staff who are faithful rather than the 10 percent who cause most of the problems.

By 1994, when *Theory R Management* was published, the proof of Alderson's effectiveness had spread far beyond Pittron. The book cited examples from his work with major corporations like 3M and Gillette, as well as from Japanese companies like Honda and Matsushita that had made similar commitments to valuing people.

Alderson delivered Value of the Person seminars at individual companies from the late 1970s to 2011, plus open-enrollment seminars in Pittsburgh and elsewhere through 2004. The seminar team typically included Alderson, his daughter, and Scumaci or Piccolo, plus colorful messages from motivational speakers like Reid Carpenter and Tony Campolo.

Alderson had a lasting impact on many companies and untold thousands of individuals. At 3M Corporation alone, for example, 2,000 employees at multiple plants received Value of the Person training between 1987 and 1991. At 3M's Little Rock, Arkansas facility, the union presented thank-you cards to management for introducing Value of the Person there. "It's the only worker motivation program that's been palatable to the unions," Scumaci told the Little Rock newspaper after a December 1989 seminar.

CONVERTING A SKEPTIC AT GRANITE CITY

In fact, American Steel Foundry initially found out about Value of the Person via labor, not management, when a representative of the boilermakers' union gave Paul Limbach copies of *Stronger Than Steel* and *Theory R Management*.

"We were really good at enforcing rules and regulations," Limbach said, "but it was evident, given our relationship with the union, that we could never become a world-class company."

After reading the books and talking to Alderson, Limbach decided to send one of his toughest, most unyielding supervisors to a Value of the Person seminar. "He came back acting completely different," Limbach recalled. "Suddenly he was being very nice, explaining things to people, and requesting input. The union even called a special meeting to try to figure out what he was up to."

Limbach sent three more of his toughest managers to another seminar. At this point, Alderson discerned that the real skeptic at American Steel was Limbach. So he called the three together at the seminar and told them, "Paul does not want to do this, and all he needs is for one of you to break ranks and he'll drop the idea." Sure enough, when the managers returned to Granite City, Limbach called them into his office individually. All three said they supported bringing Value of the Person to American Steel.

At the first on-site seminar, Limbach and union president David Spellmeyer, who had been barely on speaking terms, reconciled and began to build a relationship. The impact of Value of the Person was so great that enough seminars were scheduled to reach nearly the whole plant workforce. Value of the Person has now been working with American Steel for 14 years and has become part of the fabric of daily operations. The collaboration has expanded to include supervisor training, ongoing workshops for "point men," and a condensed one-day seminar to deliver the message to new hires right away.

Limbach highlighted two practical changes that Value of the Person brought to his leadership and to plant operations. First, he realized that "I was being very aggressive with the 10 percent and never spending any time with the 90 percent"—that is, focusing on the complainers rather than helping the majority of employees to excel. Second, he discovered that building quality relationships with workers yielded a major change in their attitudes toward innovation, because now "the people trust us enough to be willing to try something and give us advice knowing that we'll listen to it." This sense of labor-management teamwork is especially important now that implementation of new technology is crucial to competitiveness; employees who formerly viewed robots as a threat to their jobs are now open to changes that could improve their productivity.

CHANGE AT 3M

Clair Murphy oversaw Value of the Person training for a thousand employees as site director at 3M's Cottage Grove, Minnesota plant. In that role, he observed Alderson's influence even at a company that was already highly person-centered.

In Murphy's view, much of the impact of the two-day seminar happened at the concluding session, which discussed how Value of the Person could affect the family. Spouses and significant others were invited to attend this session and hear what the employees had learned.

To reach all plant employees, Cottage Grove held eight seminars. Along the way, Murphy noticed the impact spreading from those who had already attended Value of the Person to those who hadn't. "You could see people picking it up like allergens," he stated. "By the last seminar, the people had already learned much of it before they got there."

As one impressive sign of how Value of the Person changed a plant manager's relationships with workers, Murphy said, he was frequently asked to speak at the funeral when a 3M employee or retiree died, because the family knew he would have something personal and positive to say about their deceased loved one.

Murphy has been retired for over 20 years, but he knows that Alderson's impact remains strong at Cottage Grove. At one party for retirees, an employee who had joined 3M after Murphy's retirement tracked him down to say thank you, asking, "Are you the person who brought Value of the Person here?"

Ray Meier, who coordinated the seminars at Cottage Grove while working for Murphy, commented, "Wayne's presentations were something to see. You could sense afterwards that people felt a lot happier than they had been." For Meier, two keys to the seminars' success were that they included both labor and management perspectives and that everyone in the plant—plus spouses—went through the same training.

WORTH HIRING TO TEACH RESPECT

Alderson's personal presence was riveting—"he would look you dead in the eye as if he was looking right through you," Limbach said—but many more people were reached indirectly through the books or satisfied customers. Wayne Thompson, who has spent a 40-year career in manufacturing for the roofing industry, was initially one of those.

"I was visiting one of our suppliers, 3M," Thompson recalled. "At the end of the tour, the plant manager gave me a copy of *Stronger Than Steel* and said, 'I don't know what you believe, but I think you would enjoy this book.'

"I read it on the plane flight home. I couldn't put it down. It helped me to see something I had kind of known all along but never fully understood—that the success I'd had up to that point was all about caring for people.

"Then I became a plant manager in Ohio and quickly found that I'd run into a buzzsaw, with all kinds of union problems. After a couple weeks I was sitting at my desk, wondering what I'd gotten into. I looked at my bookshelf and there was Wayne [on the cover of *Stronger Than Steel*] staring at me.

"I think the Lord told me to call this man. We talked twice and he decided to come to Ohio and look at what was going on in the plant. After that he said, 'We can turn this around, but we need to have a Value of the Person seminar.'

"Convincing my boss that we needed to pay someone to teach us how to respect each other was a long conversation. But eventually we had the seminar with Sam Piccolo and his wife, Wayne and his wife, and Nancy Jean. It was terrific, it brought people together like never before, and the plant improved.

"Later I accepted a job with another company and was gone for five years, then this company brought me back. When I returned, people who had previously been skeptical told me with great sincerity that they had realized the long-lasting benefits of what Value of the Person had done for them personally and for the plant."

Thompson has distributed copies of *Stronger Than Steel* widely throughout the roofing industry. He also credits Alderson with encouraging him to become a public speaker and tell his own inspiring story: Thompson was illiterate, teased, and mistreated due to severe dyslexia until a fifth-grade teacher took enough of a personal interest in him to discover his problem.

Alderson taught Thompson another memorable lesson on a late-night stroll through the plant. "Let's walk around until we find someone doing something right," Alderson said. When they encountered an employee lining up shingles with precise care, he approached the man. "I'm visiting here," he said, and I just recognized how much you care about your job and how well you want to do it. This is the most beautiful section of inventory I've ever seen." He then turned to Thompson and said, "I think you should write a note about him, send it to his home, and put it in his personnel file." To make sure that Thompson didn't forget, Alderson had him handwrite and mail the note before they went home that night.

The following week, the employee tracked down Thompson to thank him. "I showed that letter to my wife and daughters," the worker said through tears. "They couldn't believe the plant manager wrote me a letter telling me how good a job I did. The only letters I'd ever received were reprimands. My wife bought a frame for your letter and we put it above our bed, and she has me read it to her every night."

Thompson said he has applied that tool many times since then, remembering Alderson's words: "It's not hard to be a leader, you just have to have a heart. When you care for other people, great things happen."

STILL A BARGAIN

Sharell Mikesell has been a huge fan of Value of the Person since 1992, when two of his employees convinced him to bring Alderson to Owens Corning where he was vice president for science and technology. Over two years, he arranged seminars for 400 staff, 200 spouses, and even a group of teenagers who had a special session with Reid Carpenter. After a long career in the plastics industry and at Ohio State University, Mikesell still thinks Value of the Person is unique—and a bargain.

"Some of the largest business consulting firms try to do something like this but they get more tied up in process," Mikesell explained. "Only Value of the Person actually gets to changing people's hearts and minds. And the cost was about one-third of what you would pay a big-time consultant."

Mikesell called the challenge to become open and vulnerable in front of his employees "gut-wrenching" but rewarding, as he saw work relationships improve through transparency and mutual respect. He also highlighted Value of the Person's unique inclusion of spouses. "Making them feel like a part of the company was a touching event," he explained. "Recognizing and addressing how baggage from home and the workplace affect each other is something that no other cultural initiative addresses. We saw several marriages revived as a result." Like Clair Murphy at 3M, Mikesell reported receiving appreciation from employees up to 20 years later for Value of the Person's enduring impact on their families.

Mikesell contended that many business productivity programs fail to achieve the best possible results because they overlook the most basic ingredient: people. "This is shown over and over at companies that have multiple plants with the same tools and knowledge but a wide range of performance outcomes," he stated. "The difference is all about how well they work together, understand each other, like each other, and know they are appreciated, valued and respected by leadership.

"Of all the organizational, motivational, and self-improvement programs I have attended in over 40 years in business, only Value of the Person effectively teaches how to address root-cause issues."

IMPACTING A FUTURE FAITH-AT-WORK LEADER

Al Erisman was a research and development director at the Boeing Company when he happened to hear Wayne Alderson on a radio interview. "It was the first time I realized how my faith could be connected to my work, beyond just acting ethically and sharing my faith," he said. "I bought a copy of *Stronger Than Steel* on the way home from work, read it all the way through that night, and called Wayne on the phone the next morning. We talked for an hour and became friends for 40 years. He changed the way I managed in my research position and how I saw my role in business."

Erisman subsequently brought Alderson to Seattle for a series of seminars and a presentation to Boeing management, discovering not only his effectiveness as a presenter but also his unshakable intensity. On one occasion, as they drove across Lake Washington between appointments, Erisman interrupted their discussion to point out Mount Rainier rising in the distance. Alderson replied without emotion, "That's great. Now as I was saying … ."

After retiring from Boeing, Erisman joined Seattle Pacific University as executive in residence and then as head of its Center for Integrity in Business. "I rarely give a talk without speaking about Wayne," Erisman stated, "and I often say that he changed my life. He showed me how to think as a Christian about labor-management relationships. People frequently come up to me after my talks and tell me that Wayne made a difference for them as well."

Erisman knew Alderson long enough to observe his ongoing commitment to self-improvement. "The principles never changed, but the seminars he gave in 2005 were very different from 1985," he explained. "References to technology showed up more."

Alderson's message was firmly rooted in biblical principles, but he had a standard answer when asked if his was a religious program. "Wayne said in every seminar that he made no apologies for his Christian beliefs," Sharell Mikesell noted, "but he always conveyed that the things we would talk about were love, dignity, and respect and how to display them. That defused any sense that the seminars were about religious conversion."

AN AMAZING MENTOR

On top of everything else, Alderson poured himself into long-term mentoring relationships of enormous depth. One of the appreciative recipients was Scott Stevens, who served as youth pastor at Alderson's church and is now lead pastor at North Way Christian Community, a suburban Pittsburgh megachurch (see chapter 10).

At Alderson's memorial service, Stevens explained that after he preached his first sermon as youth minister at Pleasant Hills, "I was approached by this intense gentleman who looked me square in the eye and said, 'That was okay. Just okay. Borderline unacceptable.' I remember seeing these laser-blue eyes and the hole in his head. I had never met Wayne before. He said, 'If you want to get serious and be a real point man, then call me. But don't call me if you can't take being pushed or challenged.'

"I got a lot of one-on-one time with Wayne, about twice a month for several years. There were moments when I wouldn't feel privileged [to have the opportunity]. He would just hammer away. He would ask a question, listen, say 'don't BS me,' and go right to the point. You couldn't do anything but tell the truth to Wayne. ... If you said you would do something for your wife or kids, he would check with the wife and kids and see if you did it. ... At the end he would always say, 'I believe in you and I love you.' I have learned more about my gifts and weaknesses from Wayne than you could ever imagine."

Michael Baileys, a U.S. army officer who grew up at Pleasant Hills Community Presbyterian Church, had a similar "brutally honest" mentoring experience that extended over 15 years. "Wayne saw the value of developing the next generation of lay leadership and decided to seize the initiative," Baileys said. "He gave tough counsel and it was a treasure. As Proverbs 27:6 says, 'Wounds from a friend can be trusted, but an enemy multiplies kisses.'

"Wayne would not let you wiggle away from your shortcomings. His mentorship bespoke a deeper level of relationship than I have experienced anywhere, even from pastors." From their many meetings at an Eat 'n Park restaurant, Baileys also remembers Alderson's generous tips, reflecting his compassion toward people who worked hard for not much money.

Paul McNulty, deputy attorney general during the George W. Bush administration and now president of Grove City College, met Nancy Jean Alderson when both were Grove City undergraduates and was invited to attend a Labor-Management Prayer Breakfast. Having heard from his daughter about McNulty's leadership potential, Alderson took the time to explain to him who was who and let him eavesdrop on some behind-the-scenes conversations.

"I see a lot of politicians who are always looking past the people they are talking to, looking for their next connection," McNulty said. "Wayne did not do that. He saw a college kid there to learn and took time to greet and encourage me, make me feel comfortable, and enable me to benefit from the experience."

McNulty remained in periodic contact with Alderson over the next two decades and intentionally applied what he learned from Value of the Person to his workplace—Capitol Hill—with remarkable results. "During the Clinton impeachment process," he recalled, "I was chief spokesman for the House Republicans. In a very stressful situation, while debating the White House spin machine and Democratic operatives, I was very self-conscious about showing love, dignity, and respect. I tried to maintain self-control in language and tone, show courtesy to my opponents, and characterize their position in such a way that they would feel they had been represented well, not misrepresented for my own advantage.

"As a result, I made good friendships with a lot of Democrats. Later, when I was at the Justice Department [and became involved in a controversy over the firing of several U.S. attorneys in 2006], time and time again Democrats would defend me and say, 'Whatever the issue is here, we don't think it is McNulty.' In fact, [Democratic Senator] Chuck Schumer became a key defender of me, because he remembered how I had dealt with him."

THE UNVARNISHED TRUTH

Alderson's mentoring style reveals perhaps his most shocking trait: his penchant for direct, fearless comments that no one else would dare to make. (Imagine telling a pastor whom you've never met that his message was "borderline unacceptable" and then inviting him to lunch.) This classic style served him well in the tense 1973 encounter that made Value of the Person possible—his clandestine meeting with union leaders that broke the stalemate at Pittron.

Sam Piccolo opened that meeting by presenting a piece of paper with the union's demands. Alderson threw the paper down without looking at it, saying, "I'm not here to talk about demands." At that point another union member broke into profanities, pulled out a switchblade, and declared, "I'm going to slit your throat!" Alderson shouted back, "Either cut my throat, or shut up and sit down!" As he recounted in *Theory R Management*, after a tense silence Piccolo said, "OK, we'll settle."

That same daring directness traveled with Alderson to other companies. Wayne Thompson recalled Alderson and Piccolo showing up for one meeting and finding labor and management in their typical positions, on opposite sides of the table. "Before we get started, I think I can offer a suggestion that would help right off the bat," Alderson said. "Obviously there's a problem here, because all the union's on one side and management is on the other side. I want you to mix it up." As he started pointing to people and telling them to switch sides, he said, "Sam, does that remind you of anything?" Piccolo picked up the cue: "Yes, it does. He did the same thing when he came to Pittron and made me sit right next to this goofy-looking man with a hole in his head."

Alderson had a knack for identifying the skeptics at seminars—typically the people sitting in the far back with their arms folded—and drawing them out. Limbach recalled a seminar at American Steel during which an employee spewed forth an awe-inspiring series of complaints about bad work conditions and supervisors who wouldn't listen to him. "What should you do in that situation?" the man challenged Alderson. Wayne paused for a moment and then, as if to sympathize with the employee's woes, responded in an astounded tone, "Man, you should just go and shoot yourself!" That answer might not have pleased the company's risk management department, but it brought tension-releasing laughter from the audience and broke down the employee's defenses, helping him to see that complaining would not make his life better. By the end of the day, the employee and Alderson were "best buddies," Limbach said, "and he came back to work as one of the more transformed guys in the plant."

In most contexts, Alderson saved his barbs for the powerful while treating workers with gentleness. "Wayne would say that when there is a broken relationship, the one in the position of power has the primary responsibility for resolving it," Erisman explained. "That is why he pushed so hard for management to take the lead in resolving labor issues. Whatever bad things the union might have done were not relevant to him, because management was in the position of power."

Erisman once recommended Alderson for a large, lucrative mediation job for a company preparing to negotiate a labor contract. But when the company told him that it would select the candidate and then introduce that person to the union, Alderson withdrew from consideration, saying that "the strategy was doomed to failure" because labor would resist the process if it didn't have a voice in choosing the mediator. The company would soon suffer a crippling strike.

Said Ray Meier of 3M, "His method was very simple, not boisterous but down-to-earth. He treated the workforce as his equals and talked on the level of the people who were there."

Alderson's daughter offered the simplest summary of how he could get away with seemingly insulting comments: "Even though he said things that were abrasive, people could tell that he loved them."

THE MESSAGE GOES ON

"It's the message, not the messenger," Wayne Alderson often said. Since his death in 2013, his daughter has been proving that. Nancy Alderson McDonnell (now president and CEO of Value of the Person Consultants; www.valueoftheperson.com) and Barbara Yogan (vice president for training and development) continue to deliver seminars throughout the United States and Canada, along with a team of colleagues who have deeply experienced the message themselves.

The Value of the Person seminar team ready for action. Left to right: Nancy Alderson McDonnell, Paul Limbach, Ed Self, Donnie Chandler, Barbara Yogan, John Turyan.

One of the team members, John Turyan, has a 35-year history with Value of the Person. Turyan took an entry-level job at the H. J. Heinz Company in the mid-1960s, obtained his undergraduate degree and MBA while working there, and eventually worked his way up to plant manager. A Cursillo weekend (see chapter 4) in 1979 brought his Catholic faith to life, and he later served as lay director for the Cursillo movement in Pittsburgh. But it took Wayne Alderson to show Turyan how to bring his faith into the workplace.

Turyan came to know Alderson in the early 1980s through two providential connections. The first was a college friend of McDonnell, whom Heinz happened to hire as a trainer. Then Turyan received a copy of *Stronger Than Steel* from a Heinz Pittsburgh factory worker who had an auto accident on a rainy night and who was comforted by the man whose car she had hit—none other than Wayne himself.

Turyan followed the same pathway as Limbach: first he sent others to a Value of the Person seminar, and then he attended himself and was profoundly challenged. "Wayne got me out of my comfort zone, which was dealing with numbers and corporate issues," he explained, "and got me to touch people. He inspired me to visit the union hall, sit down with workers, and talk about our families."

Turyan introduced Value of the Person to Heinz plants in Pittsburgh and Holland, Michigan and saw great results: "Communication improved, long-term resentments were dropped, and cooperation between production and maintenance employees improved, as well as between management and union officials. Our focus on employees contributed to a turnaround in previously declining business performance."

Turyan became a speaker at Labor-Management Prayer Breakfasts and a close personal friend of Alderson. He had retired to Florida and had not participated in a seminar for many years when McDonnell, shortly after her father's death, called and asked him for help in continuing Value of the Person. Turyan agreed to assist and quickly discovered that the message was still powerful even without Wayne. He came to see himself as called to fulfill a statement that a Catholic priest had made to Alderson during a small-group retreat 20 years earlier: "Value of the Person must continue some day without you."

Other seminar presenters come from American Steel, which Turyan calls "the Pittron of this generation": Limbach, retired lead supervisor Ed Self (ironically, one of the hardliners whom a still-skeptical Limbach sent to investigate an Alderson seminar), plant manager Donnie Chandler, and several unionized employees.

"The journey is going on, thanks to the team of committed presenters who, each in their own way, have been prepared for this role over the last 40 years," McDonnell said. "The message is touching hearts and changing lives, and we are all deliverers of it."

McDonnell herself, however, was unquestionably the ideal person to lead what her father had begun. "Any father would dream of having a daughter as devoted as she has been," said Paul McNulty. "It is really a further demonstration of Wayne's credibility, because nobody knows a man better than his wife and children."

When she first graduated from college, McDonnell felt called to help her father. Now she believes that she was called to even more—that God was preparing her to carry on what her father started.

McDonnell and her team continue to demonstrate that the Value of the Person message is just as powerful without the original messenger. "In every organization we assist," Yogan noted, "results have been remarkable, from employee engagement to productivity improvement—all as a by-product of doing what is right."

At the same time, some aspects of Wayne Alderson can only be revered, not reproduced. Many of his admirers stress that his personal effectiveness was inseparable from his personal history as a point man in Germany and at Pittron, from his experience of the sacrifice of Red Preston, and from the unmistakable, disconcerting hole in his head.

Stan Ott, longtime senior pastor at Pleasant Hills Presbyterian, recalled a time when Alderson, sitting in the front row, stared at the communion table rather than looking at Ott throughout his message. "I found that somewhat bothersome," Ott said. "When I talked with him afterwards, he said that during the whole sermon, he was looking at the communion elements and thinking of Red Preston. For everyone else, that was a nice war story; for Wayne, even 50 years later, it was an intensely vivid reality. He knew what it meant to have someone give his life for him. It was a humbling moment for me."

Wayne Alderson will never be replicated—and given his unusually blunt, hauntingly intense ways, probably no one would want to try. But his example and his message remain as compelling as ever. By applying Christian truth to his business life, Alderson rejected the prevailing assumption that adversarial labor-management relationships were the norm. His heroic commitment to the men of Pittron demonstrated his credibility and earned him a platform for the remaining 40 years of his life. Through the generosity, attentiveness, and sensitivity he displayed to those in need, he disarmed critics, won over skeptics, and taught thousands of people to value themselves and others as God does.

Seven

GREAT PLAYERS, GREAT MESSENGERS:

THE SPIRITUAL LIFE AND INFLUENCE OF THE SUPER BOWL–ERA PITTSBURGH STEELERS

Ted Petersen came to the Pittsburgh Steelers to play football, not to find God. He ended up doing both.

Like many star athletes, Petersen thought he was a big deal through his college years. "I lived and breathed football," he said. "I set lofty goals for myself like being co-captain, earning a game ball, and becoming an All-American. By the end of my senior year, I had achieved all those goals, but there was still something missing. I was a big man on campus, but not a big man inside."

Petersen wasn't likely to look for the answer to his emptiness in church. He had attended church with his mother as a child, but with "a Tom Sawyer mentality. I didn't know what it was all about. I couldn't wait to get back outdoors in my play clothes. If we had to sing five stanzas of a hymn, I would almost faint." As a ninth-grader, he quit going to church "because my mom couldn't make me go any more. I didn't think that was what real men did. They hunted, fished, and played football."

While achieving NCAA Division II All-American status at Eastern Illinois University, Petersen impressed a Steelers scout enough that coach Chuck Noll flew in personally to see him work out. Petersen had converted from tight end to center, and the Steelers liked having versatile athletes on their offensive line. He impressed Noll too and became Pittsburgh's fourth-round draft choice in 1977.

That meant a transition from being a star to fighting for a job. Many fourth-round picks never get past the preseason.

At training camp, Petersen met another really big man: offensive tackle Jon Kolb, who would twice place fourth in the "World's Strongest Man" contest. The two quickly became friends. "He was a real cowboy from Oklahoma," Petersen recalled. "He'd host players at his farm for archery practice, deer hunting, and trap shooting on Mondays after a game. I figured that if I did everything he does, maybe I can make the team." Except the weightlifting, of course: "We went in the weight room and he lifted 405 pounds eight times. I could have maybe done it once."

To Petersen, Kolb was the epitome of a man's man. So it was a bit disorienting when he discovered that this muscular man who hunted, fished, and played football also had a Bible in his dorm room at training camp.

Eventually Kolb invited Petersen to the team's chapel services, which he found more engaging than the rural church with five-stanza hymns. In week 11 of the Steelers' regular season, before a game in New York, the chapel speaker was Paul Eshleman, who led the Jesus film project for Campus Crusade for Christ.

As he listened to Eshleman's message, Petersen realized that "what God did at the cross was not an accident. I had gone through life believing in God's existence, and I had heard many times that Jesus died for me, but at that point it went from knowledge in my head to knowledge in my heart."

Much of Petersen's early spiritual formation took place around his football team. In the late 1970s, about half the Steelers attended chapel services and more than a dozen were involved regularly in Bible studies.

Petersen still remembers the chapel service before the January 1979 Super Bowl, at which Steeler players, contrary to common caricatures of Christian athletes, prayed that whoever could best give God the glory would win. "I wasn't comfortable with that," he admitted with a smile. "Here were 16 veteran team members sitting around me with two Super Bowl rings [from the 1974 and 1975 seasons] and I wanted one."

Petersen eventually got two rings. He also went to Florida with several teammates on an evangelistic trip, challenging college students to arm wrestling and then giving his testimony. He participated with fellow Steelers in staffing a Christian-based summer football camp for highschoolers; in fact, Petersen said his younger brother traces his spiritual beginnings to the guidance he received from Steelers safety Donnie Shell at that camp. And three decades after football, Petersen continues to receive invitations for public witness.

"I'm giving my testimony later this month at a men's gathering," he said when interviewed in fall 2017. "God blessed the Steelers with four Super Bowls in six years. That gives guys like me a platform, even today."

The 1970s Steelers are remembered as one of the National Football League's greatest dynasties. Their offense opened holes for running backs and their Steel Curtain defense tore apart opposing teams. But they should also be remembered for the holes they filled in people's hearts.

A DISTANT COUSIN COMES IN HANDY

The Steelers were by no means the only team with vocal Christian players in the 1970s and 1980s; when Petersen went to a conference for Christian athletes after his rookie season, he found about 100 other NFL players there. But the intensity of the Steelers' spiritual life during their dynasty years is remarkable. Much of it was stimulated by a young chaplain who wasn't supposed to come to Pittsburgh.

In 1974, Hollis Haff, a staff member with Campus Crusade's Athletes in Action ministry, was asked to become part of a pioneering outreach to pro sports. Until then, Athletes in Action was best known for assembling teams of former college and professional athletes who would travel around the country playing exhibition games (often beating major college basketball teams, for example) and give their Christian testimony at halftime. Now the ministry wanted to try to embed spiritual leaders as chaplains with professional teams.

Haff, a native of Bellevue, Ohio, was originally assigned to Cincinnati with a partner, but his supervisor decided that they didn't need two people in one city and asked where he might like to go instead. Haff suggested Pittsburgh, since he knew he had a distant cousin living there named Jon Kolb.

"I had met him only once in my life," Haff said, "but his grandmother would send us clippings about him from Oklahoma. I called Jon and explained what we were doing, and he said it sounded fine. That gave me one warm body to serve, so we came to Pittsburgh. My task was to penetrate the Steelers as a Christian missionary."

Although Haff encountered plenty of challenges, he also found an unexpectedly receptive mission field. Kolb, then in his sixth year with the Steelers, helped with introductions. Quarterback Terry Bradshaw, a Southern Baptist by background, also befriended Haff and boosted his credibility with the team. They would share breakfast on Mondays and then Haff would volunteer to catch passes for Bradshaw, who wanted to do a little throwing on the team's off day.

Building on this initial support, Haff began offering midweek Bible studies and a chapel service on Sundays before the team's pregame meal. The program quickly bore fruit.

"A lot of the players had some church background," Haff explained, "but when they started hearing someone teach the Bible in a way that made sense to them, they eagerly embraced Christ. Many of them experienced a transformation, and chapel grew to 25 or 30 players.

"It was clear to me that God was doing something. I was 25 years old and under-equipped biblically, spiritually, and in life, but God was able to overcome my shortcomings. There were so many strong personalities on the team that once God got hold of them, they began to influence each other."

Steeler players recall Haff not only as a skilled teacher who brought the Bible to life for them, but also as an effective discipler who challenged the players by setting up ministry opportunities for them and helping them share their faith sensitively in their public appearances. "Hollis got us out of our comfort zone," said Tunch Ilkin, who became a Christian in 1982 after his second season with the team.

Unlike later Steeler chaplains, Haff did not travel with the team, but his Campus Crusade connections enabled him to provide first-rate chapel speakers like Eshleman before away games. Before one of their Super Bowl victories, the Steelers listened to renowned pastor and writer Chuck Swindoll. "What a gift it was to hear such godly men," Petersen stated, "although Hollis was as good a speaker as any of them."

One of the most unlikely converts was Ernie Holmes, a Steel Curtain defensive lineman and a wild man both on and off the field. In 1973, Holmes, distraught when his wife left him, fired gunshots at trucks and a police helicopter, earning a weekend in jail, two months in a psychiatric institution, and five years of probation. One Sunday morning in 1975, Holmes wandered unintentionally into a chapel service. "He thought he was walking into the pregame meal," Haff said. "He sat down and then realized there was no food. A little embarrassed, he decided to stay. He kept coming back and eventually gave his life to Christ. He was still rough around the edges, but something clearly happened to him."

Hollis Haff and wife Karen with Steelers Ernie Holmes and Loren Toews and Loren's wife Valerie.

Haff had little direct contact with Steeler leadership, but he said that coach Noll personally thanked him for the difference he was making in Holmes's life. Holmes became an ordained minister after football and was pastor of a rural Texas church when he died in a car crash in 2008.

"Ernie was the outcast on the front four [of the defensive line]," recalled defensive back J. T. Thomas. "But then when they were doing public engagements, he was the one calling them to prayer. The outcast had become a leader. It was something to see Dwight White, L. C. Greenwood, and Joe Greene scurrying to join Ernie for prayer before they signed autographs."

UNITY OFF THE FIELD, SUCCESS ON THE FIELD

Except for some legends surrounding the Immaculate Reception, no one claims that God loves the Steelers more than any other team. But many of the 1970s Steelers believe that the spiritual revival that began in 1974 contributed to the team's on-field success by building tight bonds of brotherhood among the players.

J. T. Thomas has a unique vantage point on that matter. He grew up under segregation in Macon, Georgia and was among the first group of black students to integrate his high school. Most football players put their uniform on and then have a teammate pull it over the shoulder pads in the back; Thomas learned in high school to place his shoulder pads inside the jersey and then put them on together, because he couldn't count on getting help from any of his white teammates.

When a Macon sportswriter contacted iconic University of Georgia football coach Vince Dooley and encouraged him to recruit Thomas, Dooley replied, "We're not ready for a black player." Florida State coach Bill Peterson read the ensuing article, called Thomas, and said, "We are." So Thomas became the first African American player at Florida State.

When he joined the Steelers in 1973, Thomas found that racial separation still predominated. The white players lived in different neighborhoods from the African Americans, and the two races rarely socialized together off the football field.

Team prayer was already an established practice, supported by coach Noll and owner Art Rooney, both strong Catholics. But after Haff became associated with the team in 1974, he started a Bible study at his Squirrel Hill apartment. Early participants included Thomas, Kolb, center Mike Webster, defensive backs Mel Blount and Donnie Shell, and wide receiver John Stallworth. Others remained on the periphery but receptive, like Dwight White, who would sometimes ask Thomas to "read a couple Bible verses for me" as he rolled over to sleep.

"All this helped the team come together," Thomas stated. "We had tough competition, but we were undergirded by a spirituality that people weren't ashamed to profess."

Thomas observed, as Ted Petersen would several years later, that the Steeler players who combined great physical strength and submissiveness to God made other people rethink their own beliefs. "Kolb and Webster were perhaps the two strongest guys on the team," he said. "No one would call them soft. But they were also saying prayers and reading their Bible. This would raise questions among other players—why do they feel they need somebody's help? Some guys started hanging around with them and reading the Bible, hoping that maybe it would make them stronger too."

Thomas sensed the bonds growing across racial lines as white players like Kolb and Webster began to ask questions of their African American colleagues, seeking to gain a better understanding of black culture, jargon, and humor. "There was an openness and honesty that came from spiritual depth and compassion," he said. (Incidentally, those bonds have endured for 40 years. Kolb cited his open, heartfelt dialogue with Thomas and Larry Brown, a Steelers tight end and offensive tackle from 1971 to 1984, when they had contrasting perspectives on the 2017 controversy over NFL players' actions during the national anthem.)

Thomas also believes that the spiritual bonds between players spilled over into a greater readiness to support and protect each other on the field. On occasions when that quickness to protect a brother led to penalties for unnecessary roughness, he said, "even coach Noll would smirk, because he could see that it was part of our unifying bond."

When asked about how the players' faith impacted their team spirit and performance, safety Donnie Shell related an incident from his rookie season. "I was on the bench for the first time in my life. My locker was right between [running backs] Franco Harris and Rocky Bleier, so the media would go right up to them (and ignore me). One of those times, I heard this big voice say 'Hey rookie!' It was Mel Blount, offering to take me to dinner. He saw I was hurting and paid attention. Mel helped me recognize my selfish attitude and think in a more team-oriented way. He explained to me that everyone had a role to play and that if we all played our role well, we would win a championship."

THE NFL'S ONLY TURKISH-BORN CHRISTIAN CONVERT

Few Steelers have parlayed their football career into more lasting visibility than Tunch Ilkin. After 14 years as an NFL player (13 of them in Pittsburgh), he shifted into broadcasting and has been a commentator on Steelers radio broadcasts for 20 years.

But Ilkin's main job is as director of men's ministries at the Bible Chapel, a large evangelical congregation in Pittsburgh's South Hills. And he has been a prominent supporter of the city's Light of Life Rescue Mission, even serving a term as board president.

That's quite a change for the only Turkish-born player in NFL history, who came to Pittsburgh in 1980 as a nominal Muslim and, by his own admission, a very messed-up person.

Ilkin grew up near Chicago and played college at Indiana State, where he can remember visiting one chapel service, but his college years were more characterized by drugs, alcohol, fighting, and emptiness. Not expecting to be chosen in the NFL draft, he wasn't by the phone when the Steelers called to say they had selected him. His mother panicked, thinking that Tunch had just been drafted into the U.S. Army.

As a rookie just hoping to make the team, Ilkin also noticed the gentleness and sense of purpose that his Christian teammates exuded. "I was really drawn to them," he recalled—"how they reached out to others and how quick they were to share their knowledge of the game. I knew they had something that I did not have.

"There were so many Christians on the Steelers, I fell in love with the body of Christ before I knew the person of Christ. I realized that my life was very shallow by comparison."

In 1981, on the plane ride home after a Monday night loss in Oakland, Mike Webster patiently asked Ilkin where he thought he would go if he died that night. Based on his Muslim upbringing, Ilkin assumed that Allah would grade his life on a scale. "I never felt I knew how I stood with God," he recalled. "But Jon, Ted, Webby, and Wolf [offensive guard Craig Wolfley] talked about God as if they knew him."

Ilkin committed his life to Christ in February 1982. He recalled that when he told Wolfley the next day, "I was shocked at how happy he was, telling Kolb 'Hey, we got another one.'"

Haff, by then an eight-year veteran with the Steelers, participated in discipling Ilkin, as did David Good, a founder of the Bible Chapel, where the Websters, Wolfleys, and Petersens already attended before the Ilkins showed up. Tunch ended up heading the senior-high ministry for six years before moving into men's ministry leadership in 2000. He has also shared his testimony along with his Steelers memories at hundreds of public appearances.

"I know Jesus and I know football," Ilkin said. "God has used those two things to enable me to serve."

DONNIE SHELL: RECEIVING FAITH AND DISHING IT OUT

Donnie Shell had a sturdier spiritual upbringing, but he still lacked a clear personal faith when he joined the Steelers in 1974. Having attended church regularly while growing up in South Carolina, he responded positively when Haff offered Bible studies and chapel services. "I met individually with Hollis too," Shell said. "I had a great interest in history, especially Bible history, so I was very curious and appreciative of his knowledge."

But Shell did not realize his own depth of spiritual need until the last weekend of December 1974, when the Steelers traveled to Oakland for the American Football Conference championship game, with a Super Bowl berth at stake.

"I was thinking back on how I had made the team as an undrafted free agent and now I was going to play in the AFC championship game," Shell explained. "But when I got to the hotel, I felt miserable. I couldn't figure out why we were getting ready to play my biggest game and yet I wasn't happy. It was so heavy on my mind, I talked to the first guy I saw in the lobby about this.

"The guy replied, 'Through all these things you are trying to reach up to God and have a relationship with him, and you can't do it.' When I heard those words, I thought I was doomed, but he went on to explain about how Jesus reached down to us.

"That night I prayed to accept Christ. The next day I went to chapel and the same guy was there—as the chapel speaker. He said that he prayed every day to be ready for God's divine appointments and I was one of them." The man was Paul Eshleman, the same Campus Crusade leader whose message would draw Ted Petersen to faith three years later.

In subsequent years, Shell became one of the Bible study leaders at preseason training camp. Other players remember his exuberance in knocking on dormitory doors and hollering "Time for Bible study!" His commitment to placing God's priorities before his own personal success was so thorough that when he first became a candidate for the Pro Bowl (the league all-star game, for which he was selected five times), Shell told God, "If it is going to take my spiritual life away from you, I don't want to make it."

Shell repaid the favor he had received from teammates like Mel Blount by investing deeply in others. Hall of Fame wide receiver John Stallworth offered these recollections at a 2018 "For Men Only" event hosted at the Bible Chapel: "Donnie had the greatest impact on me. We both came in the same year from HBCUs [historically black colleges and universities] and grew together as rookies. I saw him accept the Lord. I had accepted Christ in grade three but didn't have him on the throne of my life. In the

Donnie Shell and Jon Kolb on stage at a men's event in the Pittsburgh area.

off-season, Donnie came to visit me in Huntsville, Alabama after a conference and wouldn't stop witnessing to me. By the third day, it started to dawn on me that I was thinking pro football was great but there had to be something else and I didn't know what it was. Donnie helped me grow in faith and Hollis taught us how to share our faith."

Shell had a particularly transforming impact on Tony Dungy, the 1970s Steeler whose Christian faith is most publicly known. Dungy went undrafted in 1977 despite a successful college career at quarterback. The Steelers signed him as a free agent, tried him at wide receiver, and then moved him to defensive back. He made the team partly because of his voracious commitment to studying strategy and game films that would later make him a great coach.

In 1978, Dungy and Shell were roommates at training camp when Dungy contracted mononucleosis and was assigned to antibiotics and rest. He didn't rest very well—Shell would come back to the dorm room and find him studying papers from the practices he was missing—but he did start worrying about getting cut.

Dungy shared his concerns with Shell, who said to him, "Tony, I think you are at a crossroads. You are so intrigued with your football preparation, I think you are putting football before God."

Retelling this exchange in his book *Quiet Strength*, Dungy wrote, "I immediately knew Donnie was right, and I felt convicted. I think that was the point at which I really began to understand what it means to be a Christian."

Dungy played only two years in Pittsburgh but joined Chuck Noll's coaching staff in 1981, the youngest coach in the NFL at that time. In 1982 he began coaching the defensive backs. About the potentially awkward situation of coaching players older than him, including his spiritual mentor Shell—just five years after showing up in Pittsburgh as a rookie who had never played defense—Dungy wrote later, "So many of them were locked into the idea of living for Christ that it didn't matter who was coaching them. They worked hard and honored God through it because that's just what they did."

When Dungy got married, Shell was his best man. When Dungy was inducted into the Hall of Fame in 2016, nine years after becoming the first African American head coach to win a Super Bowl, he chose Shell to introduce him.

As his last full-time job, Shell developed a spiritual life center at Johnson C. Smith University in Charlotte, North Carolina. He continues to coordinate the Donnie Shell Scholarship Foundation, which provides tuition assistance for students attending his alma mater, South Carolina State University.

THE QUIET STRONG MAN

Jon Kolb is the inverse of Tunch Ilkin: he uses his Steelers platform too, but in a quiet, less visible way. One colleague said you could share a long plane ride with him and probably never find out that he played football. Indeed, Kolb hesitated to be interviewed for this chapter until he was convinced that the focus would be on spiritual influence, not yet another rehash of his playing days.

Kolb grew up in Ponca City, Oklahoma, in a culture where "if you didn't play football, your parents put you up for adoption." He heard the gospel plenty, as the town's five Baptist churches each held annual revivals. Kolb says that one young friend got saved 23 times.

Kolb had a stronger understanding of faith by the time he joined the Steelers in 1969. One positive influence was his roommate at Oklahoma State University, Terry Brown (who would score the Minnesota Vikings' only touchdown against the Steelers in Super Bowl IX). Nevertheless, he says that the 1974 arrival of his distant cousin Hollis Haff made a big difference in his life too.

Jon Kolb (right) and fellow Steeler Mel Blount promoting Kolb's nonprofit rehabilitation organization, Adventures in Training with a Purpose.

"Hollis came and taught us Scripture," Kolb recalled. "I can remember his teaching from Philippians 2 to this day. At chapel and at midweek Bible studies, there was always a challenge to grow. He also exposed us to speakers like R. C. Sproul. *The Holiness of God* [Sproul's classic] influenced me more than any book other than the Bible."

Kolb was a Steelers strength, conditioning, and defensive line coach for 10 years after ending his playing days in 1981. But whereas most fitness trainers view working with elite athletes as the pinnacle of their profession, Kolb eventually perceived a calling to serve "people with greater improvement potential"—specifically, veterans of military service and people with disabilities. He got a master's degree from Slippery Rock, worked at an orthopedic clinic, and then started his own nonprofit, Adventures in Training with a Purpose. On the day of our interview, he had just spent 90 minutes helping a teenage auto accident victim learn to walk again. Kolb also leads an after-school program for about 70 at-risk youth in Farrell and Sharon, Mercer County.

HUMBLE USERS OF AN ENDLESS PLATFORM

"When you are Super Bowl champions, people want to listen to you," said Donnie Shell. As a result, over four decades the Steelers have had thousands of typical public appearances at schools, churches, and banquets—plus some nonstandard ones, like the Florida evangelistic trip that Petersen recalled.

"We would go into a bar and get on stage," he said. "Craig [Wolfley] would bend a steel bar with his teeth and then give his testimony. The next day I would arm-wrestle college students and give my testimony."

Probably the most intense shared investment these athletes made in young lives was a Christian camp that they and Haff conducted for 11

In these photos from an evangelistic outreach on a Florida beach, Ted Petersen (with hat on) takes on a challenger in arm wrestling and Craig Wolfley (facing camera) prepares to break a board with his head.

years (1976 to 1986) at Geneva College in Beaver Falls. Unlike the pattern at most camps, the star players didn't just make brief appearances; they personally coached, ate with, and lived with the campers for four days, sharing their lives and testimonies along with their football knowledge. Each Steeler had about a dozen high-school players assigned to him, and the groups would eat together and hold discussion groups between football sessions.

Kolb described one incident that epitomized the power of this selfless approach to camp leadership: "I was always nervous about kids sneaking out of the camp dormitory, so I would walk the hallways at 2:00 a.m. One night I heard a kid on the telephone with his back to me. I walked up quietly, intending to grab the kid and tell him to get in bed. But as I approached I could hear him saying, 'Mom, you won't believe this. Today John Stallworth played catch with me. I ate dinner with him. Right now he is asleep in the room next to me.' I tiptoed back to bed. The next day John was going to share his testimony, and you can bet that kid would be listening."

Attending these camps powerfully impacted the lives of two of Geneva College's most visible current staff members: Geno DeMarco (Geneva's

Discussion groups at one of the Steeler camps at Geneva College. Jon Kolb (left) is praying with the group in the foreground.

John Stallworth gives instructions to a Steelers summer camp participant.

football coach since 1993) and college president Calvin Troup, both of whom played football for Geneva in the early 1980s. "Their Christian mission superseded their professional status," DeMarco said of the Steeler players. "They had every right, as highly successful athletes, to be different from the rest of us, but they treated their professional accomplishments as secondary to their heartfelt desire to promote the gospel. Seeing how they impacted young people at the camps inspired me to become a coach."

"Unlike how the media often represents athletes, these guys were articulate Christians," Troup commented, "men of deep faith who wanted to share it in very clear ways. And so they put themselves in a position, as Jesus always did, for other people to live and eat with them. To hear men at the highest level of their sport teach the Bible to high-schoolers and talk about the impact of Jesus Christ on their lives was really dramatic."

Troup was severely injured (and his Geneva football teammate and best friend Eddie Hartman was killed, the night before his wedding) in a car accident in May 1983. Heavily medicated in a hospital room and battling to survive, Troup was surprised to see two massive bodies enter the room—Kolb and Webster. "The trauma nurses just let them come in," Troup recalled. "Afterwards they admitted that they didn't know who the men were, but they didn't want to tell men of that size to get out." Ilkin and Wolfley joined Kolb and Webster on a second visit while Troup was recuperating at home.

"Those relationships were a huge encouragement in a time of distress," Troup said. "Our connection wasn't football, it was Christ."

On a less intense level, these Steelers made hundreds of high-school appearances, challenging school staff to competitions like tug-of-war, relay races, and sit-ups and then speaking briefly about their personal lives. Haff said that the players had more latitude than other people to refer to their faith in public schools, due to the virtually irresistible lure of Super Bowl champions. When objections were raised in one case, at Altoona Area High School, the administration moved the event to the nearby Jaffa Shrine Center and said that students could have release time to attend; practically the whole student body walked down the street to hear the Steelers.

REMEMBERING MIKE WEBSTER'S FAITH

The late Mike Webster is widely remembered for two things. He was arguably the best center in NFL history: a seven-time league all-star, enshrined in the Hall of Fame after 17 years in the league, 15 of them as a Steeler. He is also the posthumous poster boy for chronic traumatic encephalopathy (CTE). Webster's was the first brain examined by neuropathologist Bennet Omalu, whose subsequent autopsies of other football players and ongoing battles with the NFL inspired the highly publicized 2015 movie *Concussion*.

Do a Google search and you'll find plenty of information on Omalu's Christian faith, but not Webster's. A lengthy 1997 *Pittsburgh Post-Gazette* article on Webster's post-football troubles made no mention of it. To his Christian former teammates, that is a gaping omission.

Webster started 150 consecutive games from 1976 to 1986 and played 220 games as a Steeler. "He did nothing halfway," said Ilkin, who was initially backup center to Webster before becoming a starting offensive tackle. "I remember a time during my second season when it looked like he got hurt. I came out to replace him and he said 'Get out of here.' I realized I would never get on the field as a center."

Terry Bradshaw, who introduced Webster at his 1997 Hall of Fame induction, said of him, "There never has been and never will be another man as committed and totally dedicated to making himself the very best he could possibly be."

Webster's determination and intensity, typified by his trademark practice of virtually sprinting to the line each time the offense broke the huddle, carried over to his spiritual life. Consistently, Christian former teammates described him as one of the team's most prominent believers, very dedicated both to attending chapel and Bible study and to his personal spiritual growth.

Leo Wisniewski, who became a Christian while playing football at Penn State and now leads a Christian men's organization in Pittsburgh, assisted Webster's group at a Geneva College football camp in 1981. "His humility really shone through," Wisniewski said of Webster. "He was a great player, but you'd never know that by the way he carried himself and how gracious he was with other people. He didn't care at all about the glamour part of football; he just loved the game."

Petersen remembered Webster as a great father and husband, "a fabulous guy who would give you the shirt off his back," and an outstanding participant at the summer camps.

But along with his intensity, teammates also observed an insecure side of Webster that became comical at times. "One year, before we played the New York Giants, I remember him listing all their Pro Bowlers and saying there was no way we could block these guys," Ilkin said. "We would call it the Webby doom-and-gloom report."

Steeler colleagues are understandably reluctant to say much about Webster's post-football years, preferring to highlight his greatness as a player and his dedication to God. Some wonder if prescription medications contributed to his dysfunction, which began to manifest itself soon after his playing days ended in 1991.

Webster died of a heart attack in 2002; Haff conducted his memorial service, pointing out that the Mike Webster of his last years was not the one he and the Steelers knew and would remember.

THE IMPACT CONTINUES: PHILADELPHIA, 2017–2018

Each of the major Pittsburgh-born movements chronicled in this book had its significance confirmed by replication. Individually and in group appearances, Christian members of the 1970s and 1980s Steelers have impacted thousands of people, and many of them have inspired the faith and ministry of later generations of players. But their distinctive experience as a great team thoroughly infused by Christian commitment was not associated with a team-level replication—until 2017.

As this book was being written, the 2017 Philadelphia Eagles rolled unexpectedly to 13 regular-season wins while featuring so many vocal Christians that the team released an official eight-minute video on its players' faith. After one of those believers, starting quarterback Carson Wentz, suffered a season-ending injury, the Eagles became the first-ever top seed to be picked to lose their opening playoff game. Instead, backup quarterback and fellow Christian Nick Foles led them all the way to a Super Bowl victory in February 2018.

After the Super Bowl, millions saw and heard the Eagles' postgame prayer led by offensive lineman Stefen Wisniewski, whose link to the Steelers dates back—well, all the way back to the day he was born. The Petersens, Ilkins, and Kolbs came to the hospital to rejoice with the Wisniewskis shortly after Stefen's birth in 1989 (and the nurses had to rebuke big, playful men for wrestling in the hallway).

Stefen's father Leo, a graduate of Fox Chapel Area High School in suburban Pittsburgh, received mentoring from Steeler players while assisting at the Geneva College camps. From 1982 to 1984, he was a starting defensive lineman with the Baltimore and Indianapolis Colts and also remained involved with the Steeler camps and other offseason youth outreach activities.

After an injury ended his playing days, Wisniewski worked in youth ministry for several years, reconnecting with Kolb while on staff at North Park Evangelical Presbyterian Church. He earned a seminary degree from Trinity School for Ministry (see chapter 8), worked in Christian higher education (he was an administrator at Waynesburg University, an hour south of Pittsburgh, when Stefen was born), and directed inner-city ministry in Chicago. He stayed in contact with his spiritual mentors from the Steelers, and when he moved back to Pittsburgh in 1997 he bought a house across the street from the Petersens.

As a result, Stefen grew up receiving mentoring as well as football guidance from Steelers of faith. In fact, his family shared several vacations with the Ilkins, Kolbs, and Petersens. Leo Wisniewski said that the group made five trips to Montana and one to Arizona, combining work at football camps with visits to national parks.

"Those trips gave us extended time together," Wisniewski stated, "for godly men to impart the weight of glory into our sons' souls in the context of real community."

Petersen moved back to Illinois in 2008, but Wisniewski continues to count Kolb and Ilkin among his closest friends and ministry colleagues, their relationships and their history of collaborating in Christian service now spanning nearly four decades.

"The day after the Eagles won the Super Bowl," Leo Wisniewski said, "when all these testimonies from coaches and players were out there and Stefen's prayer was circulating on video, it hit me that this must have been like the spirit of those great Steeler teams, except that the Steelers didn't have Facebook or YouTube."

A TRUE BAND OF BROTHERS

The degree to which players from the Steelers' dynasty years remain in public demand is not surprising. They could go into a Steelers sports bar in almost any major U.S. city, introduce themselves, and become instant objects of adulation. Indeed, given the fanaticism of Steelers fans, they might be recognized before they even introduced themselves.

The Steelers featured in this chapter stand out in several ways, the most basic of which is their unshakable commitment to using their platform to glorify God, not themselves. Their participation on one of the most famous collections of athletes ever to play football has opened doors for the rest of their lives, but they have not let it define them.

These players' submissiveness and humility are also reflected in the extent to which they have sought to let God shape them. They know the Bible thoroughly, quote it freely, and express themselves maturely. Knowing that high visibility also brings high exposure, they display clear accountability to God and to other believers.

Finally, their devotion to each other, 30 or 40 years after they stopped playing together, is truly remarkable. Many of them stay in regular contact and support each other's events. Shell lives in South Carolina, but when interviewed in March 2018, he said that he would be in the Pittsburgh area three times in April for events involving his teammates, including a large Christian men's outreach event with Wisniewski and six Steelers participating.

This chapter may still not make the Steelers popular in Baltimore, Dallas, or New England, but the stories of how men of faith have used their ongoing public platform for God's glory should warm the heart of every Christian football fan.

Eight

THE LITTLE SEMINARY THAT COULD:
TRINITY SCHOOL FOR MINISTRY

Upon entering the Trinity School for Ministry library in Ambridge, Pennsylvania, one sees an open area to the right, designated as the Stanway Africa Alcove in honor of the school's founding dean. Against the back wall of the alcove, as is common at organizations interested in world mission, a map of the world is posted. But this is not a typical map—relative to most representations of our planet, it is upside down. Africa and South America dominate the viewer's attention in this arrangement, with Europe and North America dangling nondescriptly at the bottom.

The map focuses viewers' eyes on parts of the world where this young, modest-sized school has made an incredible impact. It is also an apt image for Trinity, which has specialized in turning things topsy-turvy. In 40 years it has grown from a tiny, unpromising outpost to a globally prominent seminary, overturning the pecking order in theological education while also playing a significant role in the reshaping of Anglican relationships worldwide as well as in world mission. Trinity's history embodies what God can do when a few gifted, determined people respond sacrificially to a widely perceived need.

OVERCOMING FUNCTIONAL DEISM

Stephen Noll was a young Episcopalian with a bright ministry future. (Episcopalians in the United States are part of the worldwide association of Anglicans—usually referred to as the Anglican communion—with the Archbishop of Canterbury as their head. They changed their name after the American Revolution, when being connected to England was not good for public relations.) Converted to Christ as a Cornell undergrad, he had earned his master of divinity degree from an Episcopal seminary in California and was active in his first ministry at Truro Church, a vibrant northern Virginia parish impacted by charismatic renewal.

Wanting to provide biblically sound teaching to the Episcopal renewal movement, Noll had been accepted to enter a Ph.D. program at Manchester, England in 1976 and study under the esteemed New Testament scholar F. F. Bruce. But he wondered how he would support his family, with a third child on the way.

Noll shared his concerns with John Rodgers, an evangelical professor at Virginia Seminary, who calmly told him, "If God is calling you, you just have to trust the Lord."

It was good advice—but little did Noll know that Rodgers was simultaneously on the other side of another very similar conversation, struggling to apply that advice to himself. Alfred Stanway, an Australian native who had been an Anglican bishop in Tanzania for 20 years, was asking Rodgers to leave his post at the Episcopal Church's largest seminary and become one of the original professors at a fledgling school near Pittsburgh.

The idea of starting a new seminary had emerged from the highly charged, ambitious atmosphere of the Pittsburgh Offensive (see chapter 5). Episcopal seminaries in the United States had been strongly affected by modern and liberalizing approaches, and the vibrantly evangelical John Guest was tired of telling promising ministry candidates that they needed to travel across the pond to his native Britain to obtain sound biblical education. In 1974, fellow Offensive participant R. C. Sproul urged Guest to consider founding a school in the United States. Guest pitched the idea to one of his wealthy parishioners at St. Stephen's in Sewickley, Nanky Chalfant, who responded enthusiastically and jump-started the project with a $250,000 gift, just as her friend Dora Hillman would do to bankroll the birth of the Pittsburgh Leadership Foundation four years later.

As recounted in Janet Leighton's excellent history of Trinity School for Ministry, Guest approached the presiding bishop of the Episcopal Church, who expressed skepticism about the need for another seminary but offered backhanded encouragement: "If you have the sense that God is calling you to do this, then even though it doesn't seem wise to me, I know that you have to go and pursue that call."

At the recommendation of John Stott, perhaps Anglicanism's most respected evangelical theologian, Guest recruited Alf Stanway out of retirement in Australia and persuaded him to become the founding dean of a nonexistent dream. Stanway arrived in 1975, intending to spend his first year hiring faculty, finding facilities, and attracting students so that the school could commence operations in fall 1976.

Thus, by late 1975, Stanway was challenging Rodgers to take a leap of faith and lend his credibility to the new, self-consciously evangelical Trinity Episcopal School for Ministry—so named to signal a departure from the heavy academic emphasis and limited preparation for practical pastoral work typical of most seminary programs.

In one sense, Rodgers was ready to take the leap. He had studied under Karl Barth, one of the 20th century's most towering theological icons and leader of the "neo-orthodox" reaction to liberal theology, at Basel, Switzerland. As an evangelical at Virginia, he felt frustrated that "we were not turning out graduates who could withstand the power of secularity. They cared about people but had no supernatural resources, because they didn't believe in the supernatural and were not confident of biblical authority." Rodgers even considered leaving the world of Episcopal education for more evangelical pastures but ultimately—"surprising even myself," he commented—declined a job offer from Fuller Seminary in California.

But in another sense, he was not ready for Stanway's recruiting visit in January 1976. By his own admission, Rodgers was theologically evangelical but, in financial matters, functionally deist; that is, he wasn't certain that God would intervene directly in his financial situation. Leighton records their conversation as follows:

> Rodgers: How can I accept such a call and place my wife and children in such a shakily financed venture?
> Stanway: Do you believe God loves your wife and children?
> Rodgers: Well, yes.
> Stanway: If he's calling you, isn't he committing himself to provide for your wife and children?
> Rodgers: Well, that is what Christ teaches, but we've never lived that way.
> Stanway: Maybe it's time to start!

Rodgers agreed to come. So did Peter Davids, a biblical scholar who had also studied under F. F. Bruce. Les Fairfield, a Purdue University history professor contemplating a career change, came as both church history instructor and student. With them as the main faculty and 17 students enrolled, Trinity opened in September 1976 in rented facilities at Robert Morris University. Rodgers, Davids, and Fairfield's credentials immediately established the school's academic quality.

As for Noll, he took the leap of faith too—more than once. After finishing his Ph.D. at Manchester, he joined Trinity's faculty in 1979. And the money never ran out, although the Trinity community lived quite frugally in its early years.

A GOD-ORDAINED LOCATION FOR PRACTICAL MINISTRY

Trinity's first leaders thought that Sewickley, home to Guest's church, would make the most logical permanent location. Sewickley was (and still is) a quaint, fashionable, well-manicured town along the Ohio River, 13 miles downstream from Pittsburgh. Historically, it had been the community of choice for managers who oversaw the big industrial operations farther downriver—the steel mills of Aliquippa and U.S. Steel's American Bridge factory in Ambridge.

God, however, obviously thought otherwise, because he firmly shut the doors to Sewickley. Some Sewickley residents, perhaps confusing the clientele of an Episcopal divinity school with stereotypical college undergrads, actively opposed permitting Trinity to move in, fearing an onslaught of noisy seminarians.

During Trinity's second year, a church building and a former grocery became available in Ambridge, by then a town in socioeconomic decline. The properties were anything but glamorous, but they were highly affordable. Trinity bought both properties and has made Ambridge its home since 1978. School leaders contemplated relocation to a more attractive site at times during the next seven years, but after Trinity was miraculously spared from substantial damage during two fires at a factory immediately behind the former grocery in early 1985, they concluded that God wanted them to stay.

Downtown Ambridge is not an ideal school location—for decades, there was no nearby recreation area—but it offered affordable housing and proved a great fit for Trinity's mission. Students gained practical ministry experience in serving the needy community surrounding them through food and clothing distribution, door-to-door evangelism, and after-school activities for children. The favorable local response to those actions led to the founding of the Church of the Savior in 1985, with Trinity student Joe Vitunic as pastor. (Until then, Trinity was an Episcopal seminary in a town with no Episcopal church.) Vitunic would serve the church for its first 20 years.

Noll found that most of the early faculty fit into their humble setting quite well. "We felt like pioneers, and we all had a radical side, so we didn't feel out of our element in Ambridge," he said. "We didn't mind carpooling in someone's broken-down vehicle. After all, the students, most of whom had come to Trinity without an endorsement from their bishop, were making sacrifices too."

Trinity eventually constructed two additional buildings on land formerly occupied by a used car lot and two stores. During the planning process, school leaders discovered the extent to which locals' initial suspicion of a religious school moving in had turned to appreciation. Trinity asked the borough council to vacate a one-block alley so that the school could develop the property. When the council refused, Trinity representatives suggested that maybe they would have to move. "Immediately," Noll recalled, "signs saying 'Save Trinity Seminary' started appearing in shop windows, and there was a big meeting at the high school with 200 people saying we were the best thing that had happened to the town in years. After all, students were getting to know their neighbors and serving them in humble ways, and buying things in their stores as well. Council promptly reversed its position."

DETERMINATION IS BETTER THAN FRUSTRATION

Alf Stanway provided remarkably disciplined, determined leadership as Trinity's first dean. His personal devotional life was fervent and fixed, as captured in one of his favorite phrases: "No Bible, no breakfast." From his long association with the Anglican Church Mission Society, he derived the principle of "start small, even while intending great things." He made money a secondary issue, believing that if one obeyed God in ministry, the money would follow.

Guided by unshakable reliance on a sovereign God, Stanway refused to become frustrated by apparent setbacks. Leighton tells of one instance when Stanway and Trinity's treasurer made an appointment to visit an available property. When they arrived, praying that God would give them unmistakable direction, they learned that the property had already been sold. Showing no sign of disappointment, Stanway exclaimed, "A clear indication!"

Stanway retired from Trinity in 1978 due to the onset of Parkinson's disease. D. A. Carson, of Trinity Evangelical Divinity School near Chicago, described visiting Stanway in Australia. By then, his Parkinson's had progressed to the point where he could not talk and had to answer questions in barely legible writing. Carson asked Stanway how, after such a powerful and productive life, he was dealing with virtually complete incapacity. Stanway had to write out his response three times before Carson could decipher it: "There is no future in frustration."

John Rodgers replaced Stanway as dean and president in November 1978. As a symbol of Trinity's hard-earned acceptance, Episcopal bishop Robert Appleyard hosted and participated personally in the installation ceremony at downtown Pittsburgh's majestic Trinity Cathedral. Three years earlier, Rodgers had shown respect for Appleyard by telling him, "If you don't want this seminary to start, I won't come." Appleyard had not stood in the way, but neither had he sent Trinity any ministry candidates while waiting for the school to prove itself. Now he told Rodgers that the Episcopal Diocese of Pittsburgh was open to him and to Trinity.

With that promise of support, and with Trinity's first students ready to graduate in 1979, the school could embark in earnest on its mission of reshaping the Episcopal Church. As historian Jeremy Bonner said of the school's opening, "For the first time since the nineteenth century, an expressly countercultural seminary had been established under Episcopal auspices." Typically, when religious organizations drift off their original moorings toward more liberal views, clergy lead the way; when Protestant denominations hold their national assemblies, the clergy display more progressive voting patterns than the laity. Trinity intended to reverse the process by sending pastorally effective, spiritually renewed, theologically evangelical graduates into Episcopal parishes.

The results were impressive. Over the next 30 years, the Episcopal Diocese of Pittsburgh moved in a markedly conservative direction, both at the parish level and at the top. The diocese called theologically charismatic Alden Hathaway—who would have lost the election without the votes of Trinity faculty—as bishop in 1981 and, upon Hathaway's retirement in 1997, chose staunchly orthodox Robert Duncan to replace him. Moreover, from 1984 to 1992 the Episcopal Diocese of Pittsburgh planted nine new churches, six of them led by Trinity graduates.

Trinity benefited in turn from the change it helped to produce in the diocese, as Pittsburgh provided a path to ordination for Trinity graduates whose home bishops, viewing them as too conservative, had not endorsed them as candidates for ordained ministry.

A TENSION-SURMOUNTING SCHOOL COMMUNITY

From its beginnings, Trinity, though solidly committed to biblical faithfulness, has had to build bridges between competing views. Some of its early leaders had been deeply impacted by charismatic renewal (which put their forms of expression significantly at odds with the more staid British version of evangelical Anglicanism); others had not. One of the founding trustees objected strongly to the charismatic practice of seeking baptism in the Spirit subsequent to salvation, arguing that it introduced a false, two-tiered view of Christian piety.

"We had some very aggressive charismatic students who brought frequent 'words from the Lord' to chapel and prayer meetings," Rodgers said. "We had to write a manual on biblically faithful openness to extraordinary gifts."

Trinity overcame potential threats to harmony by remaining anchored in classic Reformation doctrine and intentionally practicing charity in nonessential matters.

"John Rodgers set the course," said "Laurie" Thompson, a charismatic Trinity faculty member since 1997 and now the school's dean and president. "He developed an ethos early on that made us all feel welcome, making it clear that neither high-church people, charismatics, nor evangelicals would be stigmatized." At moments of internal tension, Rodgers would call the Trinity community to refocus. "We knew something was going on," Thompson recalled, "when John walked into class singing 'Seek ye first the kingdom of God.' We learned to pray."

Trinity's constant effort to keep Bible, tradition, and subjective inspiration in balance is reflected in its carefully worded motto: "Evangelical in faith, catholic in order, Spirit-led in mission."

Legitimate differences of opinion are welcome at Trinity; creating disorder is not. Rodgers related one occasion when four female students came to his office and presented him with a list of written demands. Rodgers gave the piece of paper back to them and defused the conflict by stating calmly, "You are looking at a dean who doesn't respond to demands. If you would like to rewrite this as a discussion piece, the faculty will be happy to talk with you."

The hot-button issues on campus change over time, but the commitment to collegiality and seeking community-wide consensus has not. Thompson encountered a new area of sensitivity a few years ago after a celebrant at a chapel service told participants where to take their children should they make noise during the liturgy. (Ironically, the gospel reading that day was "Suffer the little children to come unto me.") The following week, a group of students brought Thompson a four-page discussion paper. "We discovered that the younger generation is very protective of children," he remarked. "It became clear that we need to include family-focused spaces in our long-range planning."

WHEN CONSCIENCES CLASH: NAVIGATING DISAGREEMENT ON GENDER ROLES

The issue of women's ordination aroused particularly strong feelings at Trinity. The Episcopal Church had voted to ordain women in 1976. For many conservatives, the decision itself was discomforting but the stated rationale, grounded more in civil rights than in Scripture or tradition, raised deeper concerns that the denomination was placing cultural considerations above theological integrity.

As a widely respected leader who had supported women's ordination while bishop of Tanzania, Stanway established a pattern of openness to Christians on both sides of the issue. Trinity accepted female students into all degree programs from the beginning, taking the position that it was a training institution, not an ordaining body, and would equip all Christians for what they felt called to do. Whatever their personal opinion, all students grew by interacting with deeply committed fellow believers who held a different view.

But keeping the peace wasn't easy. When Mary Hays arrived as

Trinity's first female professor in 1989, teaching pastoral theology, some students opposed to women's ordination declined to take communion from her or to attend chapel when she was preaching. "They would hold their own morning prayer in the chapel basement," Hays said, "so I had to walk right past them to hang up my vestments."

Hays endured that difficult experience because she understood that the dissenters from women's ordination were seeking to follow their conscience. She believed in Trinity's mission and was convinced that to function effectively, Trinity needed to be open to multiple points of view.

"The Scriptures are not univocal on women's roles," Hays stated, "so someone who is thoughtful and biblically grounded could have a different view from me. I think they are wrong, but that is not the same as saying you can't have a different position."

Hays stayed at Trinity for nine years before becoming an assistant to Bishop Duncan; Trinity has had at least one woman on its faculty at all times since then. Interestingly, Trinity got a two-for-one deal when Hays came. At Rodgers's encouragement, her husband, Whis, created a youth ministry training organization, Rock the World, and spent two years developing what became the first Anglican master's degree program in youth ministry anywhere in the world. He directed the program as a Trinity faculty member from 1991 to 2006, modeling his curriculum on the work of Gordon-Conwell professor Dean Borgman (Reid Carpenter's cousin—see chapter 5). Whis Hays estimates that more than a thousand teens found Christ through the retreats that he and Trinity students coordinated during those 15 years.

GRACIOUS IN TIMES OF DIVISION

Trinity and its faculty played prominent roles in the intense debates that would ultimately divide the Episcopal Church. Noll was Trinity's academic dean in 1987 when the Episcopal Church sent proposed new liturgies written in inclusive language (i.e., avoiding the use of male pronouns when referring to God) to its 11 seminaries for comment. "If we don't express our objections, no one else will," he told the faculty. Noll

TRINITY SCHOOL FOR MINISTRY

The Trinity faculty, decked out for the school's 1989 graduation ceremony. Left to right: Ray Smith, Pat Reardon, Doug McGlynn, Stephen Noll, Terry Kelshaw, Steve Smith, John Rodgers, Robert Munday, Les Fairfield, Jim Davis, Rod Whitacre, Mike Henning.

received approval to write a paper representing Trinity's views on language for God. Trinity students also reviewed the liturgies and submitted their responses, although the denomination declined to count them officially since Trinity decided not to actually use the texts for worship.

In the early 1990s, Noll entered the fray again, drafting a document on the Anglican doctrine of Scripture at the request of a Trinity board member who was on the Episcopal House of Bishops' theology commission. Then in 1996, John Howe, Bishop of Central Florida and previously on staff with John Guest at St. Stephen's, asked Noll to write briefs for the church trial of Bishop Walter Righter, who had been charged with knowingly ordaining a homosexual for ministry. Many conservatives in the Episcopal Church believed that the trial was their last chance to reverse the liberalizing tide in their denomination.

Noll prepared two briefs, on church doctrine and church discipline, for the Righter trial. He also coordinated Trinity's response in 1997 when the Episcopal Church asked seminaries for their opinion on "same-sex blessings" of homosexual couples.

After Righter was acquitted, conservatives in the Episcopal Church began to consider creating alternative affiliations. They had formed the American Anglican Council in 1996 to advocate for classical biblical doctrines, but up to this point they had still sought to work within the Episcopal denomination. Now, increasingly viewing that course as fruitless, they turned overseas, where their positions were still overwhelmingly supported within worldwide Anglicanism. In fact, the Lambeth Conference (the international convening of Anglican bishops, held every 10 years) of 1998 had declared homosexual practice incompatible with Scripture by 526 votes to 70.

In January 2000, some Anglican conservatives took a bold step by consecrating two Americans, including John Rodgers, as missionary bishops under the authority of archbishops from Rwanda and Singapore, respectively. The purpose was to offer alternative ecclesiastical oversight to Episcopalians in the United States. This action was controversial even within conservative circles, as it directly challenged the Episcopal Church's structure of diocesan oversight. But the approval of practicing homosexual Gene Robinson as bishop of New Hampshire in 2003 solidified evangelicals' desire to pursue new affiliations.

In this context, Trinity and its alumni took on an increasingly strategic role. According to Duncan, then Pittsburgh's bishop, "the national leadership exercised by Trinity alumni was such that two-thirds of those who were on stage at A Place to Stand [a fall 2003 conference organized in response to Robinson's ordination] were Trinity grads, giving encouragement to the more than two thousand orthodox attendees gathered from all across the United States."

In 2008, Duncan indicated his intention to remove the diocese from the Episcopal Church and align it with the Anglican Province of the Southern Cone, which comprised six South American countries. (Tito Zavala, a Trinity graduate, was Bishop of Chile within this province and would serve as presiding bishop of the province, now known as the Anglican Church of South America, from 2010 to 2016.) Before the diocese could act, the Episcopal bishops called a special meeting and removed Duncan from his position.

Within two weeks, the Pittsburgh Diocese voted 240–102 to withdraw from the Episcopal Church and align with the Southern Cone; another month later, it elected Duncan as its bishop. Remarkably, the margin in favor of withdrawal was greater among clergy (79 percent) than among lay participants (63 percent). Trinity School for Ministry—which removed the word *Episcopal* from its name in 2007—played a major role in this result.

Also in 2008, more than a thousand conservative Anglicans met in Jerusalem for the first Global Anglican Future Conference (GAFCON), with Duncan representing North America and Noll serving on the conference's statement drafting committee. GAFCON's website reflects how heated the rhetoric had become, explaining that the conference occurred because "moral compromise, doctrinal error and the collapse of biblical witness in parts of the Anglican communion had reached such a level that the leaders of the majority of the world's Anglicans felt it was necessary to take a united stand for truth."

While holding firmly to evangelical convictions about Scripture, Trinity has always sought to serve all concerned parties with grace. In 1992, it invited proponents of a liberal, social justice–oriented Episcopal magazine, *The Witness*, to celebrate their publication's 75th anniversary at Trinity, where they engaged in honest but respectful dialogue with their hosts. It remains an approved Episcopal seminary and continues to receive Episcopal students, although members of the Anglican Church in North America (ACNA), founded in 2009, outnumber them.

Duncan, who served as the ACNA's first archbishop through 2014, has been a Trinity trustee since 1996 and has taught the school's Introduction to Anglican Worship course since 2017.

AN EXPANDED GLOBAL PROFILE

The tensions within the worldwide Anglican communion had an upside for Trinity that no one could have planned: they made the school famous in Africa.

With Stanway at its helm, Trinity had African connections—and a few African students—by its second year. Its very early establishment of a two-year master of arts in religion program, alongside the three-year M.Div. degree required of American seminarians seeking ordination, helped to attract overseas students too. But the global connections mushroomed as ecclesiastical conflicts in America burnished Trinity's image as the best option for African Anglicans wishing to study in the United States.

In 1996, the Archbishop of Uganda, Livingstone Nkoyoyo, visited Trinity and expressed his desire to expand an existing theological college in his homeland into a full-blown Christian university. In 1997, he asked Noll, Trinity's academic dean, to become its vice chancellor (equivalent to the university president in U.S. parlance). Noll said he would pray about the possibility, but he and his wife didn't get around to visiting Uganda until two years later. By the end of that trip, they sensed that God was calling them. "I wrote to the archbishop," Noll explained, "saying that I will come under the condition that this will be a Christian university not just in name but in substance." By fall 2000, he was the vice chancellor of Uganda Christian University (UCU). He would stay for 10 years as the school grew to over 10,000 students on four campuses.

Even though they felt called to Uganda, the Nolls wondered why; after all, Steve Noll knew how to manage a theological school, but not departments of engineering, law, or business. But he knew one crucial thing very well: how to obtain accreditation, which he had overseen at Trinity. In 2001, the Ugandan government passed legislation giving private universities a path to accreditation; three years later, UCU became the first institution to meet the requirements.

At UCU, Noll replicated much of what he and his colleagues had done at Trinity. Departing from the Ugandan academic system, which followed the British emphasis on college as a place for professional specialization, he introduced four foundation courses in Bible and Christian thought, drawing directly from Trinity's syllabus for two of them. "The Old Testament course I constructed in 1990 has been taken by hundreds of Americans and thousands of Ugandans," Noll pointed out. He

TRINITY SCHOOL FOR MINISTRY

Stephen and Peggy Noll with Archbishop Livingstone Nkoyoyo, the man who recruited the Nolls to Uganda Christian University, and wife Ruth at Trinity in 1999.

also developed an "Instrument of Identity" document that went beyond a simple statement of faith, encompassing morals and spirituality along with essential Christian doctrine. He met with each faculty member, just as he had seen John Rodgers do at Trinity, to discuss their faith commitment and secure their affirmation of the identity statement. Noll believes that UCU was only the second university in all Africa to take such steps.

Actions that made Trinity an epicenter of global mission included the creation of the Stanway Institute for World Mission and Evangelism in 1989 and the relocation of two mission organizations to Ambridge: the South American Missionary Society (now the Society of Anglican Missionaries and Senders, with a broader global reach) in 1988 and the New Wineskins Missionary Network in 1990. John Macdonald, a 1986 Trinity graduate, further invigorated this emphasis when, after 12 years as a missionary to Honduras, he joined the faculty in 2002.

Macdonald was profoundly shaped by two Christian leaders featured earlier in this book. He grew up at St. Stephen's in Sewickley and

Henry Orombi, who succeeded Livingstone Nkoyoyo as Archbishop of Uganda, awarding degrees at a Uganda Christian University graduation ceremony. Stephen Noll is at left; at right is the guest of honor, Queen Sylvia of Buganda (one of the traditional tribal monarchies contained within modern Uganda).

committed himself to Christ under John Guest's youth ministry. During his college years, he frequently drove 65 miles to the Ligonier Valley Study Center on summer evenings to learn from R. C. Sproul.

Macdonald enjoyed a highly mission-oriented environment when studying at Trinity in the 1980s, but when he returned as a professor in 2002, the Stanway Institute's initial energy had waned. Not until several months later, when he inquired about taking a group of students to Uganda for short-term mission, did Macdonald learn that he had a travel budget. But after the watershed moment of Gene Robinson's ordination, forming a network of recognizably orthodox mission agencies that Global South archbishops could trust became a high priority. Macdonald became Trinity's "secretary of state," representing the school about six times a year in international contexts and building a huge set of contacts.

The crisis in the Episcopal Church actually helped Macdonald overcome the sense of paternalism that often pervades First World mission efforts in Africa. When preaching in Uganda shortly after Robinson's election, Macdonald said, "For decades, white Europeans and North Americans have told you that they are the experts and that you need to learn from them. But now I come to you with hat in hand, because you are the guardians of the historic, biblical Christian faith. We need your prayers and support."

Macdonald sees relationships between American and Global South Christians as mutually beneficial. On one hand, areas of the Global South where Christianity is growing rapidly have demonstrated expertise in evangelism; on the other hand, Americans offer a higher level of theological training, which Macdonald considers especially important today as theological liberalism and shallow versions of the prosperity gospel compete for adherents.

Another influential ambassador for Trinity in Africa was Grant LeMarquand, who served as a missionary in Kenya before joining the Trinity faculty in 1998. From 2012 to 2017, LeMarquand was Bishop of the Horn of Africa (which includes Ethiopia, Somalia, and Eritrea). Stationed near Ethiopia's border with Sudan, he and his wife Wendy, a medical doctor, responded to the spiritual and physical needs of thousands of refugees from the Sudanese civil war and established a theological college there. LeMarquand has since resumed teaching at Trinity.

Trinity now requires all M.Div. students to participate in at least one overseas mission trip, typically two to three weeks long, which can include preaching, leading Bible studies for adults or children, or mentoring local ministry candidates. Recent destinations have included Kenya, Tanzania, and Indonesia. In addition, Trinity funds scholarships for about eight international "Stanway Scholars" each year.

In 2008, Qampicha Daniel Wario, a Stanway Scholar from northern Kenya, told a classmate that the best way to bring the gospel to his home community would be a Christian school. Two years later, they started sharing the idea with others at Trinity, and interest grew rapidly.

Macdonald traveled to Kenya to confirm that community leaders would back the project, discovering that coincidentally, an Anglican priest with a similar vision had been raising animals on a small plot for 20 years to protect it from Kenya's land expropriation policy. With initial support coming entirely from Trinity students and alumni, the school opened on that property in 2011 and now enrolls 450 students in grades K-8, about 80 percent of them from Muslim families who value the high-quality education regardless of its Christian component.

In 2016, Qampicha became Anglican Bishop of Marsabit. His territory, ironically, bordered that of one of his Trinity instructors, Bishop LeMarquand.

Trinity is also delivering both online and on-site instruction to Nigerian theological students in partnership with the Christian Institute of Jos, Nigeria, led by Bishop Benjamin Kwashi, a Trinity doctoral degree holder and board member. Kwashi has said that Africans used to aspire to go to Oxford or Cambridge, England for theological training, but now they all want to drop the C and go to Ambridge.

In September 2018, Macdonald (newly retired from Trinity and intending to devote himself more fully to international theological training) and Noll met with the archbishop of Rwanda to discuss revitalizing a seminary there. It was *déjà vu* for Noll when the archbishop said, "I want one of you to be my vice chancellor."

AMBASSADORS FOR ANGLICANISM TOO

Trinity's motto as "an evangelical seminary in the Anglican tradition" hints at its dual identity. It promotes evangelical conviction among Anglicans, but it also promotes the treasures of historic Anglicanism to evangelicals, many of whom tend not to appreciate liturgical worship and find little value in church history between the first and 16th centuries.

Trinity upped its game on this front in 2012 by attracting the Robert E. Webber Center for an Ancient Evangelical Future, named for the late evangelical Anglican theologian and longtime Wheaton College professor, to Ambridge.

Center director Joel Scandrett, who also teaches historical theology at Trinity, was a perfect fit. He had been ordained by the American Anglican Council and placed under Robert Duncan's oversight, making him "canonically resident" in Pittsburgh even before he moved there. But beyond that, his presence and that of the Webber Center have helped Trinity to strengthen its liturgical formation of students, balance the evangelical and catholic elements of Anglicanism, and attract young evangelicals interested in reclaiming the tradition of the early church so as to renew today's church.

The Webber Center holds an annual Ancient Evangelical Future Conference and is also developing resources to improve catechesis—that is, sound training, firmly rooted in church tradition, in Christian doctrine and practice. Its longer-term plans include training courses in catechesis and a lecture series in early Christian studies.

Scandrett sees Trinity as capitalizing on evangelicals' recovery of the church fathers, an emphasis that Webber prefigured in his book *Evangelicals on the Canterbury Trail*. His writings have helped to raise Trinity's visibility in the U.S. evangelical community, along with those of faculty colleagues like Wesley Hill, a first-rate New Testament scholar who has also written about his gay sexual orientation and his commitment to celibacy.

Scandrett's efforts to promote traditional Anglicanism and Trinity in a broader ecumenical context are bolstered by two interesting partnerships. The North American Lutheran Church, a breakaway from the mainline Evangelical Lutheran Church in America, has its own seminary administrative center collocated with Trinity; its students are overseen by two Lutheran professors on the Trinity faculty, one of whom is the North American Lutheran Seminary's president. In addition, the Evangelical Presbyterian Church's Presbytery of the Alleghenies has partnered with Trinity as an approved seminary; faculty member and EPC pastor Rich Herbster serves as director of Presbyterian studies.

"The Lutherans are happy because we are more sacramental than other evangelical schools," Thompson stated. "And the Presbyterians—with whom our polity is very much in line except for who has the authority to appoint pastors—know they are free to express their leadership in their own style as well."

Herbster indicated that the EPC benefits from having a theologically compatible, geographically convenient educational partner that values the planting of new churches and the intentional training and formation of Christian leaders. "They're not on the Canterbury trail," he said of the approximately 10 Presbyterian students at Trinity, "but they take a greater appreciation of liturgical worship into their ministry and their personal devotions."

PERSPECTIVES FROM RECENT STUDENTS

Austin Gohn graduated from Northgate High School just outside Pittsburgh; his father pastored the nondenominational Bellevue Christian Church, and Austin joined that church's staff after his undergraduate study. When he began considering seminary and a friend told him about Trinity, he visited Wikipedia to find out what Anglicans are. Gohn wanted a school that was theologically conservative but not too insular; Trinity met his desires perfectly, even though his background was so low-church that when Robert Duncan, then ACNA presiding bishop, came to campus to visit with students, Gohn asked him, "What's a bishop and why do we need them?"

By his third year, Gohn knew the Anglican *Book of Common Prayer* well enough to step in and assist with leading evening prayers on short notice. He hopes that one day the curriculum might include a nondenominational track without the current handful of required courses on Anglican history and theology. (Presbyterian and Lutheran students avoid that inconvenience because Trinity offers alternative courses rooted in their traditions.) But he has gained an appreciation of the liturgical year that he said will permanently impact his preaching, especially at Lent and Advent.

"One of my closest friends in Bellevue is an Anglican priest," Gohn stated. "My personal network now goes far beyond my nondenominational circles, and I can relate to other Christian traditions easily because of my Trinity experience."

Robert Osborne, a cradle Episcopalian raised in Connecticut, worked internationally on human rights and relief issues and kept running into people connected to Trinity—Stephen Noll in Uganda, a professor at Oxford, Anglican priests in Nigeria. When he decided that his human rights discourse needed stronger theological underpinnings, Trinity was the logical choice.

As an Episcopal Church ministry candidate, Osborne represented Trinity at various events hosted by other Episcopal seminaries, where his experiences led him to a surprising conclusion: "At Trinity, you have the freedom to think differently." Some might have assumed exactly the reverse—namely, that freedom of thought would be more restricted at the most evangelical seminaries. But Osborne observed that whereas the more progressive schools tend to develop their own orthodoxies to which everyone is expected to adhere, at Trinity, within the boundaries of classical theological orthodoxy, all economic, political, and social views are welcome.

Osborne treasured Trinity's "beautiful community" of students who lived in low-budget houses all over town, with their doors open to each other and to their Ambridge neighbors. Some of his classmates took people battling addiction into their homes; Osborne volunteered on the borough's beautification committee and assisted refugees in Pittsburgh. "I heard a lot of sermons at other schools about caring for refugees," he said, "but Trinity actually does it."

Rosie (last name omitted for security reasons), a New Zealand native, found the healing experience she needed at Trinity after doing relief and development work in the Middle East during the Arab Spring upheavals of 2011 and thereafter. She also appreciated studying at a school where instructors "get emotional in class when talking about the nature of God. It is not just heavy theology—it touches their heart."

Because of its focus on training Christian mission leaders, Trinity faculty embraced Rosie's penchant for writing essays as if speaking directly to the Muslims who had asked her about Christ amidst the Arab Spring turmoil. Trinity challenged her to "let the [biblical] text create your world" rather than the reverse, she said.

As of September 2018, Rosie was returning to New Zealand to be ordained a deacon. In the Anglican tradition, she noted, "Deacons take the presence of Christ outside the church. Trinity has prepared me to do that."

AMAZING GROWTH

As these student profiles illustrate, Trinity's student body is incredibly diverse geographically, socioeconomically, and denominationally. Its growth has also been impressive. Official 2016–2017 statistics indicated a total enrollment of 199, ranking Trinity second behind only Virginia among Episcopal seminaries. This figure counts only those enrolled in degree programs; hundreds more participate in online coursework or come for special courses during brief sessions in January and June.

The "Jan and June terms" have become effective feeders into the residential programs, as students who spend three weeks experiencing the Trinity community usually want to come back for more. Short-term visitors help to sustain a new hotel constructed immediately adjacent to the seminary—an economic boost to Ambridge.

Generous scholarship assistance makes Trinity more accessible. The average Trinity student pays less than one-third of the total tuition cost; Justyn Terry, the dean and president before Thompson, energetically raised funds to provide full-tuition scholarships to five new domestic students each year, in addition to the overseas students supported by endowment monies. "It is immoral to send students into ministry with huge debt," Rodgers stated flatly. Thanks in large part to this financial aid, the average age of Trinity students, now 34 and dropping, is much lower than at most seminaries.

LEARNING FROM A GREAT RIDE

Trinity School for Ministry happened because gifted people with big visions exercised faith in a big God. But it didn't come easily. Even John Rodgers, of whom the middle-aged Scandrett said that "I want to be like him when I grow up," could trust God theologically but not financially until Alf Stanway jerked him out of his comfort zone.

Stanway lived by the dictum that "money follows ministry"—in other words, serve people well and the funds will come in. But Trinity has also reduced its dependence on money by not spending lavishly. The school purchased two buildings in a humble location and deployed considerable sweat equity to renovate a former grocery. Today, Trinity's three buildings plus a chapel across the street actually look like a small campus, but for the first 20 years Trinity was a brave outpost amidst urban blight.

Unintentionally, the school's appearance may have strengthened its spiritual intensity by causing those less firmly devoted to their call to look elsewhere. To paraphrase from Samuel's anointing of David (1 Samuel 16:7), some prospective students may look at outward appearance, but the Lord looks for committed hearts.

Trinity's story shows that there is no contradiction or conflict between spiritual fervor and academic excellence. The quality of scholars it has consistently attracted to its faculty dispels any suspicion that Trinity maintains an outmoded or anti-intellectual worldview. "We are not fighting contemporary knowledge," Rodgers explained. "We use critical scholarly tools, but we do not marry them to anti-supernaturalist principles." In fact, Rodgers turns the anti-intellectual arguments against skeptics, claiming that "there is nothing more ridiculous than a reductionist worldview."

However, Trinity has looked beyond academic credentials and theological orthodoxy, selecting instructors who also have a deep pastoral concern for enabling students to apply Christian truth to their own lives, their ministries, and the society around them. That combination of priorities has enabled Trinity to enjoy a close-knit learning community from its beginning (Rodgers described the initial faculty as "a crazy, happy group, starting a new thing and believing that the money would come in") to today. "We had our regular faculty prayer meeting yesterday," Thompson said when interviewed for this book, "and nobody left for 10 minutes after it ended. We are a family who care for each other."

Mary Hays similarly described Trinity as a "place of prayer," recalling the occasion when the whole school suspended classes and went to the chapel to pray for a student's seriously ill wife (who recovered). Her interactions with faculty at other seminaries reinforced her sense that Trinity's intense emphasis on prayer and spiritual formation is both invaluable and distinctive.

Many American and European Christians struggle to make meaningful investments in economically needy areas of the world without appearing to be patronizing. This problem is particularly acute in theological education. In this regard, Trinity has found a silver lining in the unfortunate division within Anglicanism, as it has enabled Americans who value Global South Christians' upholding of biblical orthodoxy to build true partnerships based on mutual appreciation.

Finally, Trinity's history illustrates powerfully that God's vision is always bigger than ours. John Guest, when seeking to launch Trinity in 1974, envisioned a school that would be a credible exponent of evangelical theology within the Episcopal Church and would function as a school for ministry rather than a seminary. That sounded ambitious enough. But he never imagined three other things that Trinity has become: a globally significant, ecumenical institution reinvigorating a struggling community.

To John Macdonald, this pattern of God doing more than we could ask or think once we take the first step of obedience should be the norm. "What Trinity is now was in God's mind from the beginning," he stated, invoking Old Testament interpretation to prove his point. "Psalm 119:105 says, 'Your word is a lamp for my feet, a light on my path.' Back then, people used oil lamps that only illuminated their next step forward; they didn't have a spotlight showing the whole path. We need to keep that visual image in mind, because that is how the Lord works."

Actually, Trinity's first 43 years read more like a roller-coaster ride through battle zones—both theological and literal—than a smooth path. But its people have never lost faith. They've had quite a trip, but God has unmistakably led them at every step.

Nine

NOT YOUR TYPICAL CASE OF RACIAL HARMONY:
BETHANY BAPTIST CHURCH IN HOMEWOOD

In 1897, five Christians organized the Bethany Baptist Church in Wilkinsburg. Four years later, when Thomas W. Anderson became pastor, there were 15 members and Sunday services were held in a small building in the borough's Crab Hollow area.

As the Bethany congregation grew under Rev. Anderson's leadership, he learned about an available vacant church building a short distance west of Wilkinsburg, which had formerly housed a German Lutheran congregation. As his granddaughter, Joanne Anderson Purcell, understands the story, two of Bethany's deacons inquired about purchasing the building but were turned down. The only reason they and the congregation could think of to explain the rejection was that they were African American.

Rev. Anderson took charge at that point. "My grandfather was very fair-skinned," Purcell explained. "He told the owners he wanted to buy the church building, and they agreed right off the bat." Only after the $5,000 transaction was complete did the sellers discover that Rev. Anderson was the pastor of Bethany Baptist Church, the same church whose deacons they had turned away.

THE BEGINNING

Bethany Baptist Church's first church building, purchased by the fair-skinned Rev. Thomas W. Anderson in 1905.

In the more than 110 years since that creative purchase, Bethany Baptist has amply returned the favor to its community, now overwhelmingly African American and generally known as Homewood-Brushton or simply Homewood. The congregation has invested generously in citywide ministry and world missions. It has been a beacon of racial reconciliation—most remarkably by calling a white expository preacher who served as Bethany's pastor throughout the civil rights years.

Bethany is also blessed with some tremendous storytellers, including four whose association with the church dates back 60 years or more: Purcell, Marion Adams, Dolores Speaks, and Floyd Cephas. They, head deacon Russell Boston (a relative newcomer, with only 24 years at Bethany), pastor William R. Glaze, and Chuck and Bobi Tame (the son and daughter-in-law of the aforementioned white preacher) have made it possible for us to tell this memorable story.

AFRICAN AMERICAN SERVANTS IN A WHITE COMMUNITY ...

Marion Adams's father moved from Alabama to Pittsburgh around 1917 and purchased a house immediately behind Bethany's building in 1921. The neighborhood was mostly Italian and German, with only a few African American families, during the years when Marion, born in 1927, grew up and attended school.

As the community became more racially mixed, formal discrimination was rare but de facto segregation became common. Adams told of encountering a slightly older white classmate after his return from serving in World War II and noticing that bystanders were staring at the two young people having an interracial conversation.

Rev. Anderson left Bethany for a church in Rochester, Beaver County (30 miles northwest) in 1909 but returned to Pittsburgh before his death in 1925. Purcell, his granddaughter, was born in 1937 and attended nearby Westinghouse High School. The community's racial makeup was rapidly shifting by then from whites of European descent to African Americans, but Purcell described it as still harmonious in the early 1950s. "Westinghouse had the city's top football team, and African Americans and whites played alongside each other without a problem," she said. "I didn't really experience racial disharmony until the 1960s."

Bethany grew in both financial and organizational stability under Rev. Clarence McFadden, pastor from 1944 to 1958. The mortgage on Bethany's building, constructed in 1927 to replace the small German Lutheran structure, was finally paid off, and McFadden insisted on starting church on time at 11:00 a.m. "Until then, church started whenever everybody got there," Adams laughed. "I always said that Rev. McFadden's insistence on organization was our preparation for Pastor Tame."

... AND A WHITE LEADER IN AN AFRICAN AMERICAN COMMUNITY

Although the church grew during McFadden's tenure, internal division eventually led to a vote to dismiss him in 1958. The following summer, while the pulpit was still vacant, head deacon Thomas Lee invited the Rev. Charles Francis Tame to talk about the mission outreach in India with which he was involved as a field representative for United World Mission.

Several Bethany members were admirers of Rev. Tame because of his local radio ministry, "The Happiness Hour," but Lee knew him personally through his work for the U.S. Postal Service at Pittsburgh's airport, where Tame would mail his audiotapes to radio stations as far away as Puerto Rico for broadcast.

According to his son, Chuck Jr. (who at age 12 was operating the projector for his father's presentations on the India mission), the deacons invited Tame to preach again the following Sunday, and he delivered one of his crisp, trademark expository messages. After the service, they invited him into a meeting room and stated, "We took a vote this week to hire you as our pastor." Tame agreed to stay for three months—which turned into 18 years.

By this time, Homewood had changed color. It went from 22 percent African American in 1950 to 66 percent in 1960. White flight was hastened by an influx of African Americans from the lower Hill District, displaced for construction of the Civic Arena. Moreover, the civil rights movement was gaining steam, three years after the yearlong 1956 bus boycott in Montgomery, Alabama.

Nevertheless, Bethany chose as its leader a white pastor who would remain there through the turbulent 1960s.

Interestingly, Tame and his wife, Dorothy, never moved to Homewood. Instead their residence—a one-acre hobby farm in Venetia, Washington County—became a sort of retreat and recreation center for Bethany youth and families. Adams has fond memories of climbing into a go-cart—with a dress on—for a joy ride on the Tames' property. (Chuck Jr. explained that he had received a go-cart one Christmas as a sort of compensatory gift after his disapproving father confiscated the son's used motorcycle.)

Pastor Charles Tame and wife Dorothy.

Even with the leadership's enthusiastic support, a strong all-black church of several hundred members calling a white pastor was striking. Adams recalled her own mother saying, "We have so many black men in the ministry who won't have the opportunity to lead a church like this that I feel a bit perplexed about voting for a white person." Adams never found out how her mother voted.

Bethany pastor Charles Tame with Marion Adams's mother, Juliette Moore (left), and Adams's aunt, Carmen Boddy (right). We don't know whether Moore voted to call Tame as pastor, but we know that she came to like him.

When they recall the Tame pastorate, Bethany members speak of Christian love that bridged racial gaps and of a deep sense of trust, exhibited—just as in the interracial friendships among Christian Steelers, described in chapter 7—in unabashed humor. Adams recalled an occasion when her father was ill and Pastor Tame made a home visit. Tame made a respectful comment to Marion, to the effect that if he were not married he would have considered her worthy of a dating invitation. She replied with a laugh, "I wouldn't have gone. Don't you know I am prejudiced?"

Chuck Jr. experienced that love as the only white teenager in a black church and again in 1967, when he returned from Tyndall Air Force Base in Florida with a young woman named Bobi. "Word had gotten around that Pastor Tame's son was getting married," Bobi Tame recalled. "We had the wedding ceremony immediately after church on Sunday and the place was packed."

Floyd Cephas, who would later serve as a transit system director and then as executive director at the North Side Christian Health Center, was a teenager at Bethany when Tame arrived. "We had a dilemma," Cephas said. "Folks were going crazy with Black Power and we were saying God brought us this white man. But [Pastor Tame] wasn't fazed a bit. He gave you the impression that he felt God had called him here and that was that, case closed."

Purcell believes that God knew what he was doing. "There were lots of people here who thought they were saved because they grew up in the church," she said. "When Pastor Tame came here and preached on 'You must be born again' and explained it so plainly, I knew what was missing in my life." A Bethany historical document puts it more formally, stating that during the Tame years "a strong delineation between church membership and salvation was emphasized."

Tame's tenure was characterized by expository teaching with sermon outlines, evangelism training for laypeople, and the congregation's growing connection to world mission. Purcell was part of a door-to-door evangelism team that even visited local bars to pass out Christian tracts.

Annual missionary conferences began in 1960 and continue to this day. There were some concerns when Bethany withdrew from a local mission board and affiliated with United World Mission, but Tame's personal gifts helped to overcome any hard feelings.

"I was playing piano for a funeral here that pastors from other local churches attended," Adams recalled, "and I could hear them talking to each other about Pastor Tame, just making little insulting remarks. But by the end of his message, they were on the edge of their seats. It was so pure, scriptural, and meaty."

During the years of civil rights agitation, including the severe riots that hit Pittsburgh after Martin Luther King's assassination in 1968, Bethany's people tried to protect Tame from potential risk, but he insisted on getting involved in community issues, saying that "God will protect me."

"He was really sensitive to the problems of blacks—maybe more sensitive than I was," Adams said. "Things would happen that I wouldn't even notice as discrimination, and he would notice." For instance, she recalled a group of white Christians who visited Bethany to hear Pastor Tame preach and wanted to visit members' homes afterwards to see their living situation. Tame deflected the request with the comment, "They live in better homes than you."

Bethany walked a fine line between engagement with the civil rights movement and keeping the gospel message preeminent. Adams said that after the 1963 Birmingham, Alabama church bombing that killed four young girls, some were upset that Bethany, unlike other black churches, made no mention of the attack the following Sunday morning. After further discussion, the evening service was dedicated to prayer and the congregation took up a collection to send to Birmingham.

Charles Tame died of a heart attack while playing basketball on December 6, 1977. According to Adams, shortly before his death he commented that it was time for Bethany to have a young African American man in the pulpit. After two years of interim leadership, that would happen in 1980.

A GODLY GREETING TO WHITE PROTESTERS

Bethany's overt commitment to racial harmony had an interesting sequel in 1988, as the precipitous decline of Pittsburgh's steel industry spawned high unemployment and a new round of angry protests. The most provocative player was the Denominational Ministry Strategy (DMS), a group of activist ministers seeking to promote their understanding of corporate responsibility.

The DMS became famous for some outlandish tactics, such as invading a children's Christmas party at Shadyside Presbyterian Church (the congregation of U.S. Steel chairman David Roderick) with water balloons containing skunk oil in December 1984 and placing frozen fish in Mellon Bank safe deposit boxes. When U.S. Steel changed its name to USX to reflect its diversification, the DMS mockingly followed suit, becoming the DMX (Denominational Ministry Extended).

In late 1987, DMX participants based at East Liberty Lutheran Church sought to use the small Redeemer Lutheran Church in Homewood as a base for social services. After Redeemer declined, a letter claiming to have been authored by Redeemer members began circulating in Homewood. The letter stated rather bluntly that although Redeemer recognized the community's desperate needs, "Those are the consequences of being a black community, and for that, we will take no responsibility, nor will we seek involvement. We are very proud of our track record as a white church in this declining black community."

Bethany was quick to respond. A January 4, 1988 newspaper article quoted Bethany deacon Richard Adams (Marion Adams's husband) as saying that Redeemer Lutheran had been open to its African American neighbors. "We're trying to turn this community around and they come in with this kind of divisive thing," Adams said of the DMX. The following Sunday, Adams was one of four African Americans who worshiped with Redeemer's congregation of 25.

Predictably, DMX representatives showed up at Bethany a couple weeks later. Cephas, who was there, recounted the event: "The men of our church went outside to talk with them. We were kind and offered to talk, but said no shenanigans [would be permitted] inside the building.

We wanted to ascertain what they felt could be accomplished by throwing fish inside our sanctuary. They turned and walked away. They probably wanted to goad us, but we didn't go out there as warriors."

Richard Allen Farmer, then Bethany's pastor, recalled some friendly advice that Richard Adams offered to DMX members during the encounter: "I wouldn't try some of that stuff here that you do in other places. We have some guys here who haven't known Jesus that long."

Bethany's archives contain a follow-up letter from a DMX representative to Farmer, requesting a meeting and expressing dismay about not being welcome. The letter described "the dark spirit which obviously is active in your congregation." Farmer replied, "Normally we are very receptive to any visitor … [you were disallowed] because of your reputation as one who would disrupt rather than appreciate and enter into the worship service. … As I have observed your behavior in the last months and your approach to ministry … I have not been very comfortable."

A GIFT TO THE CITY

Like the church's gracious but firm response to the DMX, Pastor Farmer's tenure itself was a gift that reverberated far beyond Bethany's own congregation. Farmer was a talented pianist, singer, and preacher all at once, holding a bachelor's degree in music from the Christian and Missionary Alliance's Nyack College and a master of divinity from Princeton. (Thanks to YouTube, you don't have to trust our description of him—you can check out his ample talents for yourself online.)

That set of non-Baptist credentials made Farmer, though ordained as a Baptist minister, a somewhat atypical candidate to lead a black Baptist church. But especially after 18 years under Pastor Tame, Bethany was not a typical church either. Farmer, still in his twenties when Bethany called him, served eight years there before going on to a ministry career of worldwide scope, which has included stops as dean of the chapel at two evangelical colleges (Gordon and Taylor). Currently, Farmer pastors a Presbyterian church in Stone Mountain, Georgia.

When Farmer arrived at Bethany, he expressed interest in forming

Richard Allen Farmer

an elite group of vocalists to give public concerts. Cephas, an accomplished drummer, convinced Farmer that they should work together, and the collaboration led to three albums featuring the "Voices of Bethany." The group debuted with a pair of rollicking concerts at Bethany—the first time drums were ever used in the sanctuary, Cephas said. With about a dozen singers, the Voices of Bethany performed at many locations in the Pittsburgh area and traveled as far as Texas and California.

For two years, Farmer (as pianist) was part of a team who led "TGIF" lunchtime events each Friday at downtown churches, with Reid Carpenter as emcee and John Guest preaching. In addition, Farmer mentored numerous seminarians and Coalition for Christian Outreach staff who served as part-time associates under him at Bethany.

Bethany generously shared Farmer's gifts with the broader Christian community by encouraging his other ministry opportunities and accommodating his travel schedule. The church benefited too, briefly moving to two services on Sundays due to growing attendance.

In one sense, Farmer never fully left Bethany, maintaining an unusual degree of ongoing investment in the congregation 30 years after his departure. He retains many personal relationships there, and numerous Bethany members have visited him at his subsequent locations.

Farmer commented that he learned how to be an effective pastor during his years at Bethany. "Those were some of the richest years of my life," he said. "I bonded with the people so significantly that even though I am physically gone from them, I maintain a vibrant and ongoing pastoral relationship with them to this day."

PASTOR GLAZE'S BIG VISION

Among the new families coming to Bethany during the 1980s were Emiel and Catrina Glaze, who initially heard Farmer at a conference and were impressed by his biblical knowledge. The Glazes became a key link to Bethany's future, because the only pastor the church has had since Farmer's departure is Emiel's brother, William Glaze.

William had a seminary degree but was an assistant football coach at Liberty University, which had just moved into college football's most competitive level, when Bethany's announcement seeking a pastor reached him. The description matched what he was looking for: a church that was serious about Bible teaching and missions-minded. The fact that his brother happened to attend there was an added bonus.

Glaze credited his two predecessors, Tame and Farmer, with laying the foundation for a church that takes Bible study and exposition very seriously. He also highlighted the unusual nature of Bethany's missions commitment.

"Very few black churches are deeply involved in global missions," Glaze noted. "African American congregations fully embrace local missions, but out of necessity—especially when the church was the rallying point for addressing racism and segregation—looking abroad took a back seat to local involvement. Also, the rise of white missionary agencies gave them a kind of monopoly in the field and tended to squelch efforts within the black community. So I was impressed that this church was supporting missions in Africa, India, and Latin America."

Bethany's world mission commitment has been embraced by the dozens of church members who have made short-term overseas trips over the last 50 years, plus three homegrown long-term missionaries: Rufus Prunty (who served for 40 years in Liberia before civil strife forced him to leave), Nancy Janet Lee (14 years in Nigeria), and Aundrae and Sheila Cassell (currently serving in Kenya).

But Bethany has not overlooked local outreach either. For many years, it was the leading provider of mentors to Family Guidance's Christian-based one-to-one mentoring program, and it has also mobilized numerous volunteers as tutors in Pittsburgh's public schools.

Under Pastor Glaze's tenure, Bethany has retained its profile as what one might call a small church that acts like a megachurch. Its current membership is about 300, but its impact on the neighborhood and the regional Christian community is far out of proportion to its size.

The most notable part of that impact today is probably the Pittsburgh Laymen's Bible Institute (PLBI). In 1994, Glaze and Swissvale pastor Maurice Doss cofounded a three-year training program in biblical counseling. In 2000, after two cohorts had completed the program, Glaze created the PLBI, adding courses in biblical studies and apologetics. In 2014, the PLBI expanded further by offering six-week courses on current issues.

Over 100 students have graduated from the PLBI; Glaze estimated that nearly half have come from churches other than Bethany. "Our tagline says we are about making a worldwide Christian impression," he noted. "We are involved in missions around the world; the PLBI is our investment right here in the city of Pittsburgh." Many graduates have moved on to pastor their own churches throughout western Pennsylvania.

Russell Boston, now Bethany's head deacon, married into the church in 1994. "When I came under Pastor Glaze's teaching, I realized that I didn't know as much as I thought," Boston said. "He has a heart for getting people to understand the Word. He wants to wipe out biblical illiteracy."

Boston completed the PLBI biblical studies program in the early 2000s and now teaches courses there. The full program lasts two to three years, with participants attending one 90-minute class per week.

Bethany is also one of the few local congregations with a regular radio presence. One of the first men Pastor Glaze discipled at Bethany, Jeff Angell, happened to be a talented producer and helped Glaze launch a radio broadcast, "Anchored in Jesus," in 1991. The program has been on the air ever since, moving to WORD-FM, Pittsburgh's most prominent station for Christian teaching, in 2008. With that move, Glaze assembled a team of Bethany volunteers to assist with the increased workload. In 2016, the ministry expanded to encompass television (Bethany's Sunday services air on Cornerstone Television's Faith and Family Channel), a website, social media outreach, and distribution of Glaze's eight books and other publications.

ATTRACTING INVESTMENT IN HOMEWOOD

In recent decades, as Homewood has sought to overcome particularly severe levels of poverty and crime, Bethany has functioned as a positive magnet, drawing substantial investment of time and money into Homewood from people who now reside elsewhere.

Boston is one of those people. A job in the North Hills caused his family to relocate to Pine Township, on the northern edge of Allegheny County, but they return to Bethany each Sunday morning. "I'd love a five-minute drive to church, but this is where God has told me to serve," he stated.

"Back in 2000, when we were outgrowing our old building and could have moved elsewhere, the vote to stay in the community was unanimous. Not only that, but when we had a choice between a church or a community center, we opted to build the latter first."

That decision enabled Bethany to receive grants from outside sources, like the Richard King Mellon Foundation, that appreciate the church's community impact but wouldn't normally give money for a sanctuary.

The congregation was also one of the many beneficiaries of the Steelers' spiritual revival. Tony Dungy, who attended Bethany during his time in Pittsburgh, made a personal contribution toward the building project and then held a fundraiser at Heinz Field. Fellow Steeler L. C. Greenwood, who died in 2013, was a quiet, unassuming, but faithful church leader. One week after hearing that the project construction cost had increased by about $200,000 during their seven years of fundraising, Bethany learned that it would be receiving almost exactly that amount from Greenwood's estate. The bequest helped to complete the fundraising campaign, and groundbreaking for the sanctuary took place in December 2017.

Football Hall of Famer Tony Dungy speaking at the Heinz Field fundraiser for Bethany Baptist Church's building expansion.

A SHINING EXAMPLE IN A RACIALLY TORN WORLD

Today, young Americans of all races learn to revere Martin Luther King Jr., Rosa Parks, and Jackie Robinson. They hear about a bus boycott in Alabama and a school desegregation battle in Arkansas. They think of the civil rights movement as a struggle that took place in the American South. Few of them realize that around the same time period, swimming pools and many other facilities in Pittsburgh were just as racially segregated as any in the South.

The most emotionally moving moments of the research for this chapter occurred when the interviewer closed his laptop and the interviewees began to retell some of their experiences outside Bethany. For example, Marion Adams described walking with a group of white friends to the nearby roller rink, where she and another black girl were picked out of the group and told they could not enter. Marion had to take two buses to Bridgeville, 15 miles away, if she wanted to go roller skating.

Adams, Purcell, and Speaks recalled their experiences of overt discrimination with a tinge of sadness (and with obvious appreciation of how America has changed since then), but without bitterness. They know better than to repay evil with evil.

People who have not experienced such blatant yet culturally established racial discrimination cannot fully grasp the anger that such injustice engenders. It is truly remarkable that Bethany Baptist Church not only eschewed malice toward America's white majority but even elected a white man as its leader during a time of sharp racial division.

Bethany's history displays the power of unexpected actions. Christians are expected to be gracious to all people, but black churches are not expected to hire white pastors, prize expository preaching, enthusiastically promote world mission, or operate an extensive Bible institute open to anyone who wishes to attend. Like random acts of kindness, such unexpected actions grab people's attention and cause them to ask for explanations, thus giving Christian believers opportunities to articulate their faith and explain how it energizes their lives.

The people of Bethany recognize that the body of Christ is bigger than one race, preaching style, or congregation. Their ministries and key decisions reflect a desire to share their gifts freely with their city and with the world. They would be the last to claim that their church is better than the many Baptist churches that surround them in Pittsburgh's East End, but their spirit of service is a magnificent model for any church.

Ten

WHEN ONE DOOR CLOSES, ANOTHER OPENS: NORTH WAY CHRISTIAN COMMUNITY

Jay Passavant, one of the most impactful pastors in recent Pittsburgh history, has his own indirect debt to Sam Shoemaker. His father was a non-practicing Lutheran who married a Catholic. When looking for a church with which they could both feel comfortable, they tried Calvary Episcopal, and Jay's father never forgot that when they came back the second time, Shoemaker greeted him by name.

Later the family moved to Beaver and Jay grew up attending Park Presbyterian Church. After college and the Marine Corps, he attended Fuller Seminary. Although theologically charismatic, he remained a Presbyterian, doing two summer internships at Memorial Park Presbyterian Church in the North Hills and then becoming student ministries pastor there in 1974.

Kathy Bain, a youth ministry volunteer at Memorial Park during Passavant's tenure there—and who is still serving as his personal assistant 40 years later—remembered him as unusually devoted to discipling youth in collaboration with their parents. "He always encouraged us to take someone along with us," she said—"even if we were just going to buy a pair of jeans, to take a girl from the youth group along and mentor her by doing life together." Another volunteer, Blaine Workman, recalled that during one winter Passavant and wife Carol invited the whole 10-member Memorial Park youth ministry team to move into their two-bedroom house for a week of community building.

By 1978, Passavant felt ready to lead his own church, but about a dozen interviews resulted in no offers. Finally, in 1980, things clicked with the search committee of a church in Suffern, New York. He was invited to preach a candidate sermon, choosing the title "If Jesus Had a Dream" for his message on the marks of an effective congregation. The church voted to accept him and Passavant promptly notified Memorial Park of his plans to leave.

In Presbyterian church polity, congregations do not call pastors independently; the presbytery (i.e., the local governing body) must approve each selection. About 10 days after the congregation's vote, Passavant received a phone call from the executive presbyter (head of the presbytery). Apparently, members of the Suffern church who didn't want him had stirred up a fuss.

"I've never said this to anyone before," the executive presbyter explained, "but it would be a tragedy for this church and your family if you take this job."

Passavant asked for time to pray. "I thought the church needed to be shaken up, but not my family," he said. Within a few days—to the great dismay of the most evangelical members of the search committee—he voluntarily withdrew.

Passavant would describe this as his "Isaac" moment. He had had a vision of founding a "vital New Testament church" in the North Hills, but he had put that vision on the altar, sacrificing it as Abraham was ready to sacrifice Isaac, to submit to God's priorities. "Once I laid that vision down," he explained, "then God was free to take over and build it." Passavant thought he should take a pastoral call elsewhere, but God had closed that door and was about to open a different one.

Around this time, some of Passavant's youth ministry team members and others who had heard about the unexpected result in Suffern encouraged him to consider launching a church. A few of them came together to pray, after which nine families committed to doing a Bible study together for six weeks. They then decided to host an informational meeting at Northway Mall, announcing it strictly by word of mouth. Passavant expected about 40 people; 90 showed up and half of them expressed strong interest.

Rather than immediately starting Sunday services, Passavant told the informational meeting, "This will be a church built around community, so if you are interested, get involved in a home group." As a result, four home groups met for two months before the first Sunday worship service took place.

Unable to secure a room at Northway Mall or a nearby hotel on a weekly basis, Passavant approached Mr. B's catering facility in Wexford. "We don't rent rooms out, we do catering," he was told. The wheels started turning in Passavant's head: "Well, how much food do we have to buy to get a room?" They agreed on a per-person price for coffee, juice, and pastries, and on March 29, 1981, North Way Christian Community held its first Sunday service with 250 people attending. (The arrangement started a long tradition: North Way continued offering food after worship services for about 20 years.) When 220 came back the following Sunday, Passavant knew a solid new church was in the making.

As the congregation grew, Passavant tried to buy the building, but the owner didn't want to sell to a church. North Way relocated to the former St. Teresa's Catholic Church in Pittsburgh's Perrysville neighborhood, but the congregation began losing people from the north suburbs who thought that the travel distance was too great.

"This was the only time in my 30 years of leading North Way when I wondered if God was saying our time was up," Passavant recalled. "But then on Easter Sunday 1985, I picked up the newspaper and saw a photograph of the Mr. B's building and the words 'For sale by auction.' The owner was facing some kind of personal crisis and had to liquidate. We ended up buying the building for about half what we had originally offered, and we got the tables, stoves, and plenty of kitchen equipment besides."

WHAT MAKES A VITAL NEW TESTAMENT CHURCH?

Starting a brand-new, independent congregation gave North Way a clean slate, and Passavant perceived both an opportunity and a responsibility to remain faithful to the model of the original New Testament church. Thousands of congregations have found their marching orders in Acts 2:42, which states that the early believers "devoted themselves to the apostles' teaching and to the fellowship, to the breaking of bread and to prayer." But North Way did so with particular rigor.

"What drove us," Passavant said, "was the idea that the early church was not primarily an organization but a fellowship, a living organism made up of people who shared a common base in Christ." That image became expressed in North Way's name, which includes the word *community* instead of *church*. The unusual word choice attracted many people's curiosity in North Way's early years, although it also occasionally aroused suspicions of cult-like activity.

North Way's intentional effort to mirror the early church community arose directly from the four values of Acts 2:42. With regard to teaching, Passavant said, "We found that even people outside the church were interested in what the Bible said about matters of life, purpose, and relationships with other people and with God." So North Way initially offered three biblically based messages every week—two on Sunday and one on Wednesday—with gifted lay leaders supplementing Passavant's preaching.

The second value, fellowship, was reflected in extensive engagement of lay participation and especially in the emphasis on home groups, which North Way has maintained in spectacular fashion for 37 years. Today, more than half of North Way's regular attenders also participate in a small group, about double the average even among congregations that promote this mode of involvement. Visitors to North Way's Wexford campus in September 2018 received a "small group connect menu" with

49 options. Reportedly well over 100 groups were in operation, but most are closed to new members to encourage a depth of sharing that often does not occur with newcomers present. The emphasis on intimate personal relationships via home groups has enabled North Way to be what Passavant called "a small church with a lot of people."

Inspired by the reference to "breaking of bread" in Acts, North Way trained its leaders to make home groups a place to share life together, not just Bible studies. "In first-century culture, meals were not something to be rushed through," Passavant observed; "they were a time when people would open up and have conversations." As on Sunday mornings, North Way prized the role of food in contributing to an open, celebratory atmosphere.

Finally, prayer was anything but perfunctory in North Way's early days, as the church—er, community—hosted an hour of corporate prayer starting at 6:00 a.m. on weekdays. It started with typical turnouts of 10 people and peaked at around 300 after North Way entered its new building in 1994.

"Regular prayer is one of the most difficult things to sustain, because things don't happen at the pace people want and they lose heart," Passavant commented. "Thankfully, we saw enough evidence of God's presence and blessing to maintain our motivation."

DEVOTED TO CREATIVE WORSHIP

North Way always featured the exuberant worship typical of the charismatic renewal, but with a clear commitment to balanced spirituality and to expressing itself in ways that would be accessible to newcomers. "My husband was probably the most demonstrative worshipper," chuckled North Way original Arlene Rink, "so Jay suggested that he sit in the back."

Worship at North Way soon became distinctive in new ways thanks to an outpouring of creativity coordinated by Jan Sherman, who was the pianist at the founding informational meeting and ended up as worship director for North Way's first 10 years.

Consistent with its desire to involve all members actively, North Way initially let a variety of people take turns as worship leader but soon discovered, as Sherman explained, that "there was a logic behind having gifted, trained music and worship leaders." After that, a regular team met weekly for worship, Bible study, and rehearsal.

Setting up each week at a catering facility brought unusual challenges. North Way's grand piano was stored during the week in a beer cooler, where the temperatures perhaps weakened the instrument's stability. One Sunday, Sherman and a guitarist were sitting on the piano bench, providing musical interludes as Passavant explained each of the Hebrew words for worship, when the piano suddenly fell in their lap, its front legs having collapsed. The sound team rushed to prop up the legs, Passavant admonished Sherman to "play carefully," and everyone survived the service.

In 1985, Sherman, worship leader Susie McCabe, and about 15 North Way members attended a national worship symposium in Pittsburgh and were overwhelmed by the dynamic applications of creative arts that they observed. Assembling gifted members who shared the vision, they began incorporating banners, processions, dance, and drama into Sunday worship.

Music rehearsal and setup for a special outdoor North Way worship service in the late 1980s.

NORTH WAY CHRISTIAN COMMUNITY

A roughly 500-member church at the time, North Way made an unusual decision. "We determined to embrace anyone who wanted to participate in the worship ministry," Sherman said. "This philosophy is a costly one. It means that you need to have training for people who are below performance standards. It also means providing resources and opportunities based on the participants' entry level.

"For example, we grew to have several dance ministry troupes. Entry-level members participated in major events and on holidays in subsidiary roles (such as in the aisles). The next level was trained to perform as a group on stage. The top-level group, composed mostly of professional dance instructors, would choreograph and lead dance groups or perform solo dances themselves." Similarly, musicians from junior-high students to professionals each had their own groups and service opportunities.

Ultimately, North Way assembled volunteer groups in 10 different worship-oriented specializations: lighting, sound, orchestra, choir, dance, drama, arts, banners and flags, stage construction, and costumes and makeup. The stage was set up differently each week—"to place a question mark in people's minds as they entered the sanctuary," Sherman said, "opening their souls to the possibilities of what might happen that day."

The worship arts teams found an inventive way to foster harmony and sensitivity to the Holy Spirit: at weekly rehearsals, everyone spent about 20 minutes together in what they called "Wild Kingdom." During that time, in an atmosphere of worship, any participant could offer a contribution as he or she felt led—a dance, song, instrumental solo, or message. The group would then discuss what moods each form of expression was eliciting, and team leaders would provide further instruction to individual contributors as deemed appropriate.

The extensive skills available on the multiple teams permitted cross-training as well—such as vocal soloists getting instruction from the drama director to help them experience and communicate more powerfully the message of their songs. "Our philosophy," Sherman noted, "was that if you change the life of the performer, you will change the lives of the people in the congregation."

North Way mobilized as many as 250 volunteers for special dramatic performances that drew up to 10,000 people over the Christmas and Easter seasons. McCabe, who served in worship leadership from 1982 to 2007, sought to ensure that the pageantry present at special events and even in regular Sunday services did not obscure the simple truths of Scripture. Congregational worship songs remained simple and easily memorizable, "so that people left with them in their heads and hearts," McCabe said.

Passavant believes that North Way's commitment to both explaining and enacting expressive worship was a big contributor to the church's early success. Repeatedly, he indicated, newcomers would tell him that their first experience of worship at North Way had moved them to tears, or that "something new happened to me."

BUILDING BLOCKS OF SUCCESS

North Way's development of creative, inspiring worship was a major attraction, but many other less visible practices contributed to an environment marked by enthusiasm, inclusion, and excellence.

"Seeker-sensitive" congregations following the model of Willow Creek Community Church designed their Sunday services for non-Christians, asking committed believers who wanted deeper instruction to attend midweek meetings. North Way never became intentionally seeker-sensitive in Willow Creek fashion, but it applied a variation on the theme by frequently using Wednesday services to discuss developments in the church's vision and direction. Key leaders attended regularly on Wednesdays, which became the time when what Sherman called "the top third of the congregation" could hear from the senior pastor on anything from new plans for expansion or children's ministry to logistical matters like seating and parking arrangements.

North Way ministry staff took periodic field trips to visit other successful congregations around the country. By reflecting on these visits, leaders could refine the church's vision and embrace new directions together rather than just hearing about changes from Passavant or the elders. For example, a staff visit to Willow Creek inspired a greater effort to integrate worship and drama elements with the sermon and convey a consistent message.

Once a year, the Passavants invited a cross-section of North Way attenders, from elders to people they'd never met, to their home for dessert and a conversation about the church. Sherman recalled seeing faces go blank when Passavant would ask, "What sermons do you remember from the past year?" and noted that the best-remembered messages were often those reinforced by visual aids or object lessons.

Passavant typically took a full month off from his regular duties each year, but before doing so he would invite prayer requests from the congregation. While away, he laid all those requests—up to 800—in front of him, not only for prayer but also to help him grasp the most prominent issues that North Way's people were facing. The trends he observed on those half-sheets of personal disclosure often impacted Passavant's selection of sermon topics for the following year, guiding him to address widespread practical concerns like praying with consistency, parenting, or representing Christ in the workplace. The requests reminded him that "people weren't struggling with the inerrancy of the Bible, but with living for Christ in a very challenging culture."

In these ways, along with its constant home group emphasis, North Way exceeded typical church practice in involving and listening to its people, thereby strengthening the social and spiritual bonds that kept participants energized and motivated to invite others.

North Way's innovative community building has even extended to its global mission efforts. Lisa Anderson, sent out as one of North Way's first "global partners" in 1983 and still serving in Honduras 35 years later, noted the church's special "homecoming" occasions every few years when it helped to pay missionaries' travel costs back to Pittsburgh so that they could share time together and experience a time of refreshment, fellowship, and camaraderie with the congregation.

NOT JUST FOR THEMSELVES

North Way's exploding worship experience overflowed to bless others around Pittsburgh, as the church began hosting regional worship symposia and also formed a fellowship of music and worship leaders from around the city. The symposia drew up to 1,500 participants who learned from instructors in all aspects of worship arts and then rehearsed together for a final performance. Two of those performances took place at Heinz Hall downtown; in the second year, 40 churches were represented and the hall was packed, with 500 people turned away.

Such multi-church events are usually hard to pull off because other churches fear losing their members—especially when the host is a dynamically successful startup like North Way, which reached an average attendance of 2,000 by 1990. Sherman was particularly touched after one such event when another North Hills pastor sent her a note saying, "I trust you with my sheep."

North Way overcame fears of proselytism, as well as jealousy of its enormous success, by displaying unmistakable forms of selfless concern for other churches' welfare. John Nuzzo testifies to the influence of Passavant's personal embodiment of this servant-like mindset. After Nuzzo started a church in Cranberry Township, about 10 miles from North Way, in 1993, Passavant invited him to join a group of North Hills pastors who met monthly. "I had little practical understanding of how to pastor a church," Nuzzo admitted. "I began to ask Jay questions, and he has been gracious in answering them for over 20 years."

One spring, before the group broke up for the summer, Passavant asked what other churches were planning for their fall kickoff. "When I said I didn't know what he was talking about, he thought I was being self-deprecating," Nuzzo explained. "But then he realized I didn't understand how to make the church more effective relationally at different seasons of the year. So he started explaining to me how to reach people at Christmas, New Year's, and so on. Today, our church is intentional about capitalizing on the seasons of life that people pass through. None of that would have happened without Jay's influence."

Victory now has about 3,000 people attending each week, and Nuzzo credits North Way with "breaking the sound barrier" by showing that a megachurch could serve people effectively in suburban Pittsburgh. He said that Passavant stands out as "a leader who is as excited about what God is doing in other places as under his own leadership."

REACHING INTO THE CITY

The same pattern of giving to others marked North Way's outreach to the city of Pittsburgh. "We believed early on that we were called to serve the city," Passavant stated. "But we realized that it takes a unique giftedness for a 98 percent white, suburban church to do that."

Relying on the Pittsburgh Leadership Foundation and others to make connections, North Way actively pursued collaborations with the Light of Life Mission and city churches interested in partnering with a suburban congregation. In 1985, it hosted a Christmas banquet for people referred

Some of the hundreds of tables prepared for one of the Christmas banquets at the David L. Lawrence Convention Center that North Way and friends fully sponsored for city ministries in the late 1980s.

by city ministries. Those attending enjoyed a meal, a musical performance, a turkey to take home with them, and a bag of additional gifts. The following year, North Way moved the event to the David L. Lawrence Convention Center. By 1989, the number of diners reached 4,000, served by 600 volunteers (most but not all from North Way). The banquets ended on that high point because the unions with exclusive service contracts at the convention center, which had generously offered substantial discounts to make the event financially manageable, felt that they could do so no longer at that magnitude.

Pastor Jay Passavant (right) with city ministry leaders at a North Way–sponsored Christmas banquet for about 4,000 urban guests. The sign behind them read, "Embracing Our City."

Passavant described these banquets as among the most God-pleasing activities of his ministry career. But in addition, North Way became valued by inner-city ministries that would typically view a suburban church as out of touch with city needs. That motivation to serve the city has especially blossomed through a partnership with the Pittsburgh Public Schools and Family Guidance, in which North Way became engaged in 2006 through a happy coincidence of interests.

Bryan McCabe (Susie's son) had just moved back from California, where he had served as a public-school teacher and administrator. While applying for jobs around Pittsburgh, he felt moved to write out a concept plan for churches to partner with schools. Meanwhile, the Pittsburgh Public Schools (PPS) and Family Guidance were launching their

Learning Assistance and Mentoring Program (LAMP), which pairs volunteer mentors from churches with specific public schools.

Around the same time, Passavant visited Pittsburgh deputy mayor Tom Cox to ask for ideas on how North Way could best serve the city. Cox offered two ideas: help businesses thrive or improve public education. Passavant chose the latter and was referred to PPS administrator and LAMP founder Errika Fearbry-Jones, who already knew him from a previous city endeavor. North Way agreed to become a LAMP partner and asked McCabe if he would be interested in helping to set up the partnership. He explored the opportunity and found that the idea "mirrored what God had given me."

When North Way announced the need for mentors willing to work with students at Faison Elementary School in Homewood, nearly 100 people signed up. As a result, McCabe never took a public school job. Instead, he moved his family to Homewood and became North Way's point person for LAMP. Now in his 13th year, he has been involved in deploying more than 500 people who have served Faison students as school- and community-based mentors.

"Suburban churches often have good intentions but then don't follow through," McCabe observed. "I was determined not to let that happen." To enhance his urban ministry skills, he voraciously committed himself to learning all he could from noted leaders like Ray Bakke, completing a training program through Bakke Graduate University.

Fear of the city, usually driven by stereotypes and exaggerated perceptions of the prevalence of crime and violence, discourages many suburban congregations' involvement. McCabe recalled that when he first went to Homewood, he gripped the steering wheel tightly and tried to avoid making eye contact with passers-by. "Once I met people, the Lord broke me of those biases," he said. "Now I drive through the neighborhood with my windows down, looking for people to say hello to.

"If you view the city as a broken place and go in trying to fix it, you will fail every time," McCabe stressed. He said that North Way combats the risk of paternalistic attitudes by highlighting the quality of city-based

Overlooking the city from Mount Washington, Jay Passavant shares with a group of Bakke Graduate University urban ministry students visiting Pittsburgh in October 2018. North Way's Bryan McCabe was the host instructor.

partners—his own two daughters attended Pittsburgh Public Schools—and the transformations that occur in the lives of volunteers, not just the students served.

MULTISITE REPLICATION

Today, North Way is actually a city church as well as a suburban one, thanks to a timely change of plans from concentrated growth at one site to dispersed growth at multiple locations.

In 2002, North Way committed over $4 million to purchase 46 acres of property adjoining its building to prepare for future growth. After worship one Sunday, attenders were invited to plant colored flags in a large pile of sand that had been dumped near route 19; each flag was to represent someone they would invite to North Way when the church built a 4,000-seat sanctuary.

The sand pile attracted curiosity, but the big sanctuary never happened. Instead, as Passavant began learning about the emerging trend of U.S. megachurches becoming multisite operations, he saw a way to reach more people without a huge capital investment. North Way examined its participant statistics and discovered that outside the immediate north suburbs, the largest cohort of attenders, comprising both urban professionals and students, was coming from the city's Oakland neighborhood (Pittsburgh's university district).

North Way ended up selling nearly all the 46 acres to commercial developers, retaining only a small portion to enlarge its existing building and expand parking. In 2008, it opened an Oakland campus, since followed by sites in the East End (with Bryan McCabe as its first pastor), Sewickley Valley, Dormont, and Beaver Valley.

North Way leaders sought to place its campuses in locations where no similar congregation existed. According to their research, no successful church plant had occurred in Oakland for at least 25 years before North Way's arrival. The East End campus has attracted young professionals drawn to the neighborhood by the influx of Google and other technology firms.

A multisite church structure requires, along with a major technology investment, campus pastors willing to pour time into relational ministry rather than preparing weekly messages. North Way's campus pastors preach six to eight times a year, but for the most part they exercise church and community leadership in other ways.

Chris White is well positioned to evaluate the nature of campus leadership at North Way, since he is not a homegrown leader. With prior church planting experience in Texas, he moved north in 2017 to become the Beaver Valley campus's founding pastor.

"What piqued my interest about North Way's system was the chance to be a campus pastor but not feel I was out there by myself," White stated. North Way undergirded the startup with a list of 35 local families who had been driving up to 45 minutes to the Wexford campus, plus a multifaceted marketing campaign that included radio, billboards, yard signs, direct mail, and social media. Moreover, White came on board a full year before the launch date so that he could learn North Way's systems, visit other campuses, become saturated in the church's culture, participate in hiring staff for his campus, and become familiar with the Beaver Valley's people and culture.

These carefully planned actions resulted in an instantly viable congregation. Beaver Valley attracted 800 people on its first weekend, in February 2018, and has averaged over 500 attenders per weekend since then.

Some of White's early actions at Beaver Valley replicated North Way's prior strategies. He promptly built collaborations with other local pastors, and he directed two volunteers to meet with the Rochester Area School District administration and find out how they could help. The conversation snowballed into seven churches helping with cleanup and simple repairs for three school districts. Rochester Area was so appreciative that it held a picnic for the participating churches.

"Multiple pastors said they have never seen congregations come together as the Church and serve like this," White said. "But we did not want this opportunity to be a one-and-done service project. We wanted to become an ongoing demonstration of God's love by serving together, affecting our culture and restoring it to God's intended design."

White has biweekly meetings with lead pastor Scott Stevens, to stay aligned with North Way's overall direction and discuss his achievement of established personal and strategic objectives, and with Passavant to capture insights from the founding pastor's long experience.

A SEAMLESS SUCCESSION

In 2011, Passavant transitioned into the role of "founding pastor" and Stevens (a beneficiary of Wayne Alderson's mentoring, as described in chapter 6) became lead pastor. In most megachurches where the founder has stayed for 30 years, the succession process is somewhere between bumpy and disastrous. Clearly things went much better than that at North Way, because (a) Passavant still attends the church and (b) he wrote a book about the transition process, *Seamless Succession*.

Passavant can describe this process with humility because, as he freely admits in his book, North Way messed up on its first attempt. The church was considering one of its teaching pastors as a candidate for senior leader, but rumors and rumblings poisoned the discernment process. When North Way started over, it put a formal transition team in place, implemented monthly churchwide communications, and made a considerable investment in evaluating four internal candidates, in partnership with an outside executive training and assessment firm. In fact, the process was so arduous that two of the four candidates contemplated dropping out along the way.

Once Stevens was selected, Passavant met with him weekly for five months prior to the formal handover of senior leadership, gradually integrating him into his new role. He then remained on the pastoral team while supporting and fully affirming the new leader. Passavant believes that his continuing but non-interfering presence helped the congregation to embrace its new leader more readily and confidently. Instead of the typical dropoff after a longtime pastor steps down, North Way's attendance increased by 15 percent in the next three years.

Passavant argues that during a leadership transition, no one is better equipped to offer insight and support to the new leader than the previous leader. But he also understands that in many cases the former pastor's ongoing involvement can seriously harm the successor's effectiveness. "If the departing senior pastor is unable to release his or her positional authority, then amputation is probably the only alternative," he wrote in his book.

Like George Washington stepping away from the presidency after two terms, Passavant exhibited a willingness to release control that made amputation unnecessary. As John Nuzzo put it, "All Jay would have had to do is talk to five or six people and exercise his influence, and it would have undermined the transition. To truly walk away from his former level of influence and let the new leadership make decisions is a rare action that reflects his trust in God."

Along with humility and grace, Passavant highlighted dedicated, daily corporate prayer as an essential component of the succession process.

The people involved, he wrote, had a deep sense that "God was in control because we asked him to be, every single day."

Passavant's ongoing responsibilities include mentoring various staff, representing North Way at local events, and general pastoral duties such as visiting or conducting funerals for people with whom he has retained personal ties. He has also further expanded his mentoring role as an evangelical participant in the Human Formation Coalition, a Pittsburgh-area nonprofit that provides spiritual formation opportunities for both Catholic and Protestant leaders.

MORE THAN MEETS THE EYE

North Way's worship services today look much like those of other evangelical megachurches. In fact, even though its lineage is charismatic and its closest analogue in Pittsburgh's South Hills, the Bible Chapel, was originally a Plymouth Brethren church—or about as non-charismatic as one can be—the two churches' services are strikingly comparable today. They have similar sanctuary arrangements, worship teams, music styles, and multimedia and lighting applications. The services at both churches consist essentially of singing, announcements, and a message, and they almost always last 65 to 70 minutes. (Passavant says that child-care demands ultimately made 90-minute services untenable.)

But if a megachurch could be boiled down to a recipe of certain essential ingredients, then anybody could make one. North Way's success is attributable to several factors to which many churches give inadequate attention.

Even as a startup congregation, North Way was stable in important ways. In a time when many charismatic churches were chasing the newest emotional fad, North Way combined a willingness to take risks with balanced positions on theological and practical issues. "Extremes lead down a destructive path," Passavant stated. Or, as original member Kathy Bain put it, "We did not want to become known for an emphasis, other than biblical teaching. Our emphasis was that we had no emphasis, except Jesus."

From day one, North Way has marvelously captured the relational nature of Christianity. It has translated the New Testament picture of a community of believers who care deeply for one another into modern life, most notably in its constant promotion of home groups but also in its discipleship and service activities.

North Way's high standards of excellence and professionalism, apparent in its creative worship and special events by the mid-1980s, persist today in new forms. Drawing from the business world's quality control methods, North Way establishes measurable Key Result Areas for each campus, and each staff member has a personal performance plan. The guest experience is carefully constructed to offer newcomers ample information and immediate contact with a campus pastor. Depth of spiritual formation remains a high priority, reflected during fall 2018 in North Way's churchwide promotion of Rooted, an experiential 10-week discipleship program.

North Way has had many exciting moments over its 37 years, but in reflecting on its history, Passavant highlighted the importance of continuing in faithfulness and obedience to God when nothing particularly memorable seemed to be happening. "There were huge time gaps between the big events recorded in the book of Acts," Passavant said. "It was the same with us. We tried to be faithful every day to what God had called us to, even when it may not have seemed very exciting. People think that spiritual transformation is an emotional experience, but lasting transformation is an ongoing infusion of the Holy Spirit, released through the daily disciplines of doing life with Jesus. That is what made North Way what it is today."

Finally, North Way's senior pastor succession experience exemplifies a central biblical principle. Jesus was willing to make himself nothing (Philippians 2:6), but church leaders frequently struggle to let go of their positions. By stepping aside when he could have been extending his senior pastor career for another decade, Jay Passavant demonstrated an awareness that the church was bigger than him and enabled North Way to continue growing in collegiality, congregational unity, and numbers while navigating its biggest transition.

Eleven

WHAT CAN WE LEARN?

Each of the previous nine chapters has closed with suggestions as to what we can learn from the great works of God chronicled therein. In this concluding chapter, we offer a few final reflections on what the whole collection of stories implies for people wanting to serve God faithfully in 21st-century Pittsburgh or any other city.

THE POWER OF ORDINARY (OR WORSE) BUT BOLD BELIEVERS

But Moses said to God, "Who am I, that I should go to Pharaoh and bring the Israelites out of Egypt?" —Exodus 3:11

It is easy to assume that when God wants to do great things, he calls great people. The rest of us take refuge in our ordinariness. Like Moses, we beseech God to call somebody else. But many of the people whom God called to change Pittsburgh were unlikely choices, unimpressive, even rejects and outcasts.

Wayne Alderson was an ordinary businessperson nagged by a sense that the typical adversarial stance between labor and management was not how things should be. Rejecting the prevailing tendencies of virtually everyone at his company, he stood up for a different paradigm. By doing so, he placed himself on a path marked by criticism, ridicule, and even dismissal. By boldly refusing to abandon the path, he changed workplaces all over America.

Reid Carpenter didn't appear to have any special gifts as he floundered through high school and was booted out of Moody Bible Institute. But he cared about reaching young people for Christ and was willing to do what it took to reach them: entering dangerous places, acting silly to get kids' attention, pleading with disarming frankness for financial support. Through a long series of obedient acts, he developed a leadership model that has impacted not only Pittsburgh but dozens of urban centers.

Don James, Tom Petro, and many other Pittsburgh Experimenters had seriously messed-up lives. To people around them, they must have seemed hopelessly irredeemable. Not only did they powerfully reflect God's grace by their redemption, but God uniquely redirected their gregariousness and social skills to touch many others.

The Pittsburgh Experiment was blessed by gifted leaders, but it was successful primarily because normal businesspeople were willing to invite friends to lunch meetings and to share their lives transparently at those meetings.

The Pittsburgh Steelers featured in this book were amazing football players, but they performed their most valuable acts only after they recognized the emptiness in their soul and committed themselves to growing as Christians. Hollis Haff felt woefully inadequate to reach a football team, but he offered his abilities faithfully and a revival broke out.

Ralph Keifer and Bill Storey were well-educated university faculty, but their greatest impact came from their willingness to learn from relatively uneducated fellow Christians like David Wilkerson and a prayer group of laypeople. The students who attended the Duquesne Weekend had no particular claim to holiness; they just wanted to know God more deeply and were willing to follow where he led them. Their willingness to step out in faith and speak boldly of the amazing things they experienced at the Ark and the Dove helped to reshape the Catholic Church worldwide.

The deacons of Bethany Baptist Church were normal people not looking for attention. They knew that calling a white man to pastor an all-black church during a period of rising racial tensions was risky. But because they believed that a white preacher was the right man for their congregation—and because, unlike many whites at that time, they had no color line—they called him anyhow.

If you want to be part of great works of God, start by making yourself ready to do whatever he asks of you.

SPIRITUAL DISCIPLINE AND INTENSE COMMUNITY

Could you not keep watch with me for one hour? ... The spirit is willing, but the body is weak. —Matthew 26:40–41

Contemporary American spirituality has tended to take on an individualized character, as professing Christians let personal preferences and busy schedules guide their involvement. Many are not connected with a local church at all; many of those affiliated with a church often limit their participation to simply attending worship, watch online, or show up irregularly. In their devotional life, they settle for brief prayer times on the way to work or when a need arises. Such people are unlikely to see God work through them in powerful ways.

The spiritual lives of the people highlighted in this book were marked by high levels of self-discipline and commitment to community. We don't know the details of all their private devotional lives, but we have plenty of outstanding examples of engagement in prayer and spiritual formation: Alf Stanway's motto of "No Bible, no breakfast"; North Way's 6:00 a.m. prayer meetings; Helen Shoemaker's prayer schools; the Pittsburgh Leadership Foundation's emphasis on prayer as necessary undergirding for its projects; Paul Everett's intensive cultivation of personal spirituality among Pittsburgh Experiment members; and the untiring commitment to biblical knowledge and instruction exhibited by Bethany pastors Charles Tame, Richard Allen Farmer, and William Glaze.

These people also lived out their spiritual experience intensely in community. Deep relationships with other believers were a constant priority for Sam Shoemaker dating back to his Oxford Group days and the core activity of the Pittsburgh Experiment. Those who experienced transformation through the Catholic charismatic renewal came together weekly to celebrate, study, share, and encourage each other. North Way presented home groups as an indispensable part of Christian life. Trinity School for Ministry succeeded partly because it created a tight community of people deeply concerned for each other and driven by a shared vision. Value of the Person turned workplaces into caring communities, with the biblical underpinnings where people were open to hearing them.

Ever since Jesus' interaction with the sleepy disciples at Gethsemane, believers in Christ have struggled with weakness in their personal devotional lives. God strengthened and did not abandon those disciples, and he shows great forbearance with our weaknesses today. But just as football championships require daily practice of fundamentals like blocking and tackling, spiritual champions must start with the fundamentals of prayer, study, and community.

A BROAD VIEW OF THE CHURCH

Accept one another, then, just as Christ accepted you, in order to bring praise to God. —Romans 15:7

One strikingly recurring theme through this book is the interdependence and mutually beneficial cooperation between Protestant and Catholic Christians.

Sam Shoemaker (even though Episcopalian, which is as close to Catholic as a Protestant can get) did not mince words about his theological disagreements with Catholicism. Yet he urged broad Christian cooperation and sought to encourage believers to strengthen whatever church they were already involved with, including Catholic churches.

The Pittsburgh Experiment welcomed Catholics as equal partners (even if Catholic laypeople needed extra prodding to pray in public) and worked closely with a Catholic outreach to the homeless.

From its very beginning, the Catholic charismatic renewal relied on guidance and mentoring from spiritually mature Protestants like Betty Schomaker, Flo Dodge, and Harald Bredesen, and it consistently welcomed ecumenical participation in its prayer meetings and local community groups.

The Pittsburgh Offensive and Pittsburgh Leadership Foundation had firmly evangelical roots, but Reid Carpenter and others realized that it would be foolhardy to try to transform Pittsburgh for God without Catholic participation. Throughout the PLF's history, evangelicals, other Protestants, and Catholics were involved at all levels. The international Leadership Foundations organization is now led by a Catholic, David Hillis, and Reid Carpenter himself has become Catholic. Amen to Action, probably the largest cooperative Christian undertaking in Pittsburgh since the 1993 Billy Graham crusade, started with an invitation from the city's Catholic bishop to Protestant leaders.

Wayne Alderson was evangelical, but the enormous impact of Value of the Person would have been impossible without the partnership of two respected representatives of the labor community, Lefty Scumaci and Sam Piccolo, both Catholic. In fact, the workers who asked Alderson to start a lunchtime Bible study at Pittron Steel were Catholics.

The Pittsburgh Steelers who experienced spiritual revival in the 1970s and 1980s, though they became or already were theologically evangelical, consistently credited their devout Catholic coach (Chuck Noll) and owners (the Rooney family) with creating a God-honoring environment that encouraged spiritual growth. And North Way's founding pastor has teamed with the Human Formation Coalition to deliver greatly valued instruction to Catholic priests as well as Protestant pastors.

There remain some conscientious dissenters today, of course, just as R. C. Sproul stands out as the notable outlier in this book. We do not wish to minimize the extent or the importance of ongoing theological differences. But from the local level to the increasingly robust collaborations between the World Evangelical Alliance and the Vatican over the past decade, Christians dedicated to impacting our modern world have recognized that we are most effective when we join hands.

A BROAD VIEW OF CHURCH-PARACHURCH RELATIONSHIPS

Now you are the body of Christ, and each one of you is a part of it.
—*1 Corinthians 12:27*

Often church congregations and parachurch organizations have had a tense relationship, marked by competition for dollars and participant loyalty. Many of the people and Christian groups featured in this book displayed an unusually firm commitment to eliminating that tension.

Sam Shoemaker recognized that the church was not the only or even the best mechanism for reaching the lost. He enthusiastically embraced such parachurch groups as Young Life and the Fellowship of Christian Athletes. He then helped to found a parachurch group in his own city, the Pittsburgh Experiment, while keeping it firmly anchored in the church by placing representatives of five downtown congregations on its original board. The Experiment consistently expressed its intent to feed renewed Christians into the churches, not to replace the church in people's lives.

Driven partly by concerns that charismatic experience could breed divisiveness or cause participants to leave the Catholic Church, the Catholic charismatic movement explicitly encouraged its adherents to demonstrate their dedication to their parish by serving faithfully, supporting parish leaders, and working patiently for renewal.

The Coalition for Christian Outreach, an early spinoff from the Pittsburgh Offensive, bridged the usual divide between congregations and campus ministries by conceiving a new model in which staff would serve both campuses and churches. That model remains intact more than 45 years later. Bethany Baptist is one of the many partner congregations that have supported Coalition staff who also worked within the church.

The Pittsburgh Steelers who received inspiration and early discipling from Hollis Haff of Athletes in Action (a parachurch ministry) committed themselves to ongoing spiritual growth by becoming involved with a local church—not an easy thing to do when you're working up to 20 Sundays a year.

Whereas financial need can often induce a narrow concentration on the survival of one's organization, when Christians commit to a broader vision such as citywide impact—as was most vividly illustrated by the Pittsburgh Offensive and Pittsburgh Leadership Foundation—those pesky church-parachurch conflicts usually disappear.

A CITY'S CHRISTIANS ARE ALL CONNECTED

Should I not be concerned about that great city? —Jonah 4:11

The theme of citywide impact provides an apt bridge to our last point, perhaps a logical one for a book that set out to collect examples of God's memorable work *in Pittsburgh*: Christians in a particular metropolitan area are unavoidably linked together. Our activities and reputations greatly affect each other's effectiveness, and often one group of Christians can provide what another group just a few miles away can use. So it is invaluable, despite the logistical challenges and potential turf battles involved, to get all Christians in a city functioning together as much as possible.

One surprising illustration of that fact is the number of ways in which the chapters in this book are intertwined. We knew about some of them before we started: Sam Shoemaker started the Pittsburgh Experiment, Shoemaker inspired Reid Carpenter, and Wayne Alderson's Labor-Management Prayer Breakfasts were one of the Pittsburgh Leadership Foundation's first projects. But there are many more examples:

- Karen Plavan, who led the PLF's addiction and recovery spinoff for many years, was deeply shaped by Shoemaker's legacy.
- The Pittsburgh Experiment's radio program featured numerous appearances by prominent Steelers—11 in one year according to a February 1980 newsletter.
- Steelers made enormous public and financial contributions to local congregations, typified by Tony Dungy and L. C. Greenwood at Bethany. (In a more recent example, Antwaan Randle

El, one week after throwing a touchdown pass for the Steelers in the February 2006 Super Bowl, was the featured speaker at the Bible Chapel, and attendance swelled from the usual 1,600 to 2,800.)
- Wayne Alderson, at a crucial point in his life, received guidance and inspiration from R. C. Sproul, who had come to western Pennsylvania as a result of the Pittsburgh Offensive.
- John Guest came to Pittsburgh to work for the Pittsburgh Experiment, cofounded the Pittsburgh Offensive, was the first director of the Coalition for Christian Outreach, and helped to create Trinity School for Ministry.
- Hollis Haff (who eventually shifted from Athletes in Action to a church pastorate) and Leo Wisniewski (the former NFL player who has collaborated with many Steelers in ministry and whose son led the prayer at midfield after the 2018 Super Bowl) got their seminary training at Trinity.
- Wayne Alderson mentored Scott Stevens, who succeeded Jay Passavant as lead pastor at North Way Christian Community.
- Several people interviewed for other chapters mentioned that Alderson's example had major impact on their own approach to functioning as Christians in the workplace.

We could undoubtedly dig up many more examples, but the point should be clear: Christians strengthen each other in a plethora of ways, so our work is impoverished—and so is our city—when we all go about doing our own things and don't foster mutual connections.

One of the most poignant moments in the research for this book came toward the end of our three-day visit with Reid Carpenter, when he asked Bob Jamison whether Christian leaders in Pittsburgh were interacting as closely as they did in the days of the Pittsburgh Offensive. Bob described some regional gatherings but depicted them as not nearly as cohesive or productive as those in the 1970s that had such lasting results. In response, Reid, in his unsettlingly probing way, wondered if perhaps this project was inspiring Bob to step forward and address the apparent need for stronger collaboration.

Regardless of who takes the lead, strong citywide connections seem to be an important ingredient in the success of most great local works of God. We hope that this book will inspire the Christian leadership of Pittsburgh to pray, serve, and collaborate so as to produce many more examples of people making Pittsburgh as famous for God as it once was for steel.

NOTE ON SOURCES

With bibliographic and other information so readily accessible today through appropriate Internet searches, the approach to documentation traditionally used in historical works, which provides publication details on all written sources, seems superfluous. Moreover, since the book is so heavily dependent on interviews and private archives, we did not want to clutter the text with unhelpful footnotes. However, we do want interested readers to know where we got our information (or at least to feel confident that we did not invent it), and we want to cooperate with researchers and others who may wish to access the same sources.

We owe an enormous debt to the interviewees who generously offered their time and insights. Without them, this book would have been impossible. By mutual agreement, all interview transcripts are confidential throughout the interviewee's lifetime, unless he or she authorizes a transcript's release.

We will do our best to answer requests for information from the media, researchers, or other interested parties. Readers wanting more detailed documentation than the text provides are welcome to contact us at Godatworkinpgh@gmail.com.

CHAPTER 2

Interviewees: Maggie Everett, Karen Plavan, Terry Webb.

The best source on Sam Shoemaker's life is Helen Smith Shoemaker's biography, *I Stand by the Door* (1967). Most of the historical information in the chapter comes from that book.

Calvary Episcopal Church in Pittsburgh and its archivist, Bob Dilts, were extremely cooperative in hosting visits for review of Shoemaker's printed sermons and other files in the church archives.

The references for the remainder of the chapter are organized below by section heading.

From privilege to personal calling. Most of this section comes from *I Stand by the Door*, 48–80 and chapter 24. "The test of a man's conversion": Shoemaker, *How To Become a Christian* (1953), 74. Nickie Shoemaker Haggart's comment is in Dick B., *New Light on Alcoholism: God, Sam Shoemaker, and A.A.* (1998), xix. Dick B. also describes the history of Shoemaker's involvement with Bill Wilson; see pages 4–5 and 363. On Shoemaker and the National Prayer Breakfast, see Peter J. Boyer, "Frat House for Jesus," *New Yorker*, September 13, 2010, www.newyorker.com/magazine/2010/09/13/frat-house-for-jesus.

Called to a second city. Moreell described his pitch to Shoemaker in a talk at Western Seminary (now merged into Pittsburgh Theological Seminary), transcribed and printed in *Western Watch*, March 1, 1958, available in the Pittsburgh Experiment archives. Shoemaker described his decision to go to Pittsburgh in "How To Know the Will of God," an essay collected in *Extraordinary Living for Ordinary Men* (1965), 46–48. Helen's version is in *I Stand by the Door*, 156–57. Shoemaker's letter to the warden is in Calvary Episcopal Church's Shoemaker Room.

Revitalizing the golf club crowd. The standard source on religious superficiality in 1950s America is Will Herberg, *Protestant-Catholic-Jew* (1955). Shoemaker's initial meeting with the golf club crowd is described in a 1955 article on the Pittsburgh Experiment by Ray Hoffman of the *Pittsburgh Press*. A typewritten version of the article is in the Experiment archives. See also Michael J. Sider-Rose, *Taking the Gospel to the Point* (2000), 19. Shoemaker on the new birth ("I am shocked"): *How To Become a Christian*, 71. Phil Ashey's recollection is at https://americananglican.org/current-news/billy-graham-well-done-thy-good-and-faithful-servant/. *Time* article: "God & Steel in Pittsburgh," March 21, 1955.

Faith as an experiment. Rationale for his method: *How To Become a Christian*, 9–10. The "act as if" method was also described in an October 1954 *Reader's Digest* article, "Act as If—The First Step toward Faith."

Getting laypeople going. Alcoholics Anonymous as a model for small groups: "The Balance of the Christian Life," a sermon preached on an occasion of preparing people for confirmation. After emphasizing to his listeners the necessity of a decision for Christ, Shoemaker encouraged becoming exposed to other Christians with deep spiritual lives through small groups. 1 Corinthians 12 ("The highly powerful"): The quotation is from "Are You a Channel of Spiritual Power?" preached on October 28, 1956.

Sam in the pulpit. The Shoemaker Room archives have records on sermon distribution; prices are also given on many of the printed sermon copies. *Newsweek* article: March 28, 1955.

The meaning of communism. The "All indifference" quotation is from a sermon called "Harden Not Your Hearts," September 30, 1956; the Castro reference is from "Charismatic People," probably 1961; "It is positively sinful" comes from a sermon titled "Christianity and This Crisis" (1955); "We are rich beyond" is from "Are We Fiddling While Rome Burns?" (n.d.).

No ducking controversial topics. The two sermons on charismatic gifts were titled "The Gifts of the Holy Spirit."

NOTE ON SOURCES

A final masterpiece on spiritual renewal. Page references, in order, for the quotations from *With the Holy Spirit and with Fire*: 22, 23, 48, 74, 53, 57–58, 30, 91, 92; see pages 80 and 105 on social concern and spiritual transformation.

He intended to pastor till age 72. Long work hours: "How Do Ministers Think of Their Work" (n.d.). Shoemaker's comments in a vestry report and in a letter to his congregation are in Calvary Episcopal's Shoemaker Room archives, as is his letter of July 1, 1963. Articles on Shoemaker's retirement event at Carnegie Music Hall are in the Pittsburgh Experiment archives. Baiz's memorial sermon, "He Who Would Valiant Be," is included in Calvary's collection of Shoemaker's sermons. On the Recovery Ministries award, see Karen Zweifel, "Rising Rates of Addiction Make Samuel Shoemaker Legacy More Relevant Than Ever," January 31, 2017, www.episcopalcafe.com/rising-rates-of-addiction-make-samuel-shoemaker-legacy-more-relevant-than-ever/.

Gracious but intense. Sermon quotations in the first paragraph are from "Our Pittsburgh Picture Today" (apparently November 1955) and "Depth and Width in Living" (probably 1959). The letter on massages is in the Shoemaker Room archives. Calvary Church retains an audio recording of the forum held on the first Shoemaker feast day. The poem is quoted from Helen Shoemaker's biography. Interestingly, there are different versions; the version in *Extraordinary Living for Ordinary Men* has "I stay near the door" as the title and refrain.

CHAPTER 3

Interviewees: Dick Bauer, Chris Buda, Maggie Everett, Kerry Fraas, John Guest, Joe Hines, Ted Kerr, Tom Petro, Jay Roy, Sue Zuk.

James's conversion story is retold in Helen Smith Shoemaker, *I Stand by the Door*, 265-72. The extended quotation is from Pat Fields, "Experiment in Daily Religion Turns Salesman into Clergyman," *Knoxville* (Tenn.) *Journal*, January 29, 1963, Pittsburgh Experiment (hereafter PE) archives. The PE archives have valuable historical reference material arranged in folders by year; unless otherwise noted, materials cited can be found in the folder for the appropriate year.

Experimenting to transform souls. Moreell's comment: "The Pittsburgh Experiment," *Western Watch*, March 1, 1958, page 11, PE archives. The launch was described in a First Presbyterian Church newsletter, PE archives. Cohea's comment appeared in his annual report of February 1957. Paul Offill's background was described in a *Charleston* (W.Va.) *Daily Mail* article, found in an album on PE director Chris Buda's desk.

New ministries flourish. The PE archives contain a collection of Oglebay conference programs. The St. Joseph director's comment was in Bill Ott, "Pittsburgh Program 'Applies' Religion," *Pittsburgh Catholic*, March 10, 1966. Jim Leckie was quoted in the PE newsletter, winter 1966. Meeman's editorial and Knoxville newspaper articles are in the PE archives.

The longest-term staffer. Everett's conversion was described by Robert Schwartz, "He Tried God in His Business Life, Now Helps Lead Experiment Here," *Pittsburgh Press*, September 23, 1967. Everett recalled his first encounter with Shoemaker in the PE newsletter upon his retirement in May 1995. Issues of the *Guideposts National Newsletter* from 1982 to 1991 are in the PE archives, as are copies of Everett's booklet *The Power of 30 Days*. The July 1983 PE newsletter reported on the pilot mixed-gender groups, which had been operating for two years.

CHAPTER 4

Interviewees: David Mangan, Tom Mangan, John Sweeney. E-mail correspondence with Al and Patti Mansfield. Background conversations with Ron Lengwin and Pat Molyneaux. Special thanks to Ray French and Tom White of Duquesne University for assistance with accessing the university's archives.

The essential firsthand source on the Duquesne Weekend is Patti Gallagher Mansfield, *As by a New Pentecost: The Dramatic Beginning of the Catholic Charismatic Renewal* (1992; expanded golden jubilee edition, 2016). Other invaluable sources on the early years of the movement are Kevin and Dorothy Ranaghan, *Catholic Pentecostals* (1969) and Edward D. O'Connor, *The Pentecostal Movement in the Catholic Church* (1971). Pentecostal historian Vinson Synan became popular among Catholics after he included a chapter on Catholic charismatics in his 1971 book *The Holiness-Pentecostal Movement in the United States* (revised in 1997 as *The Holiness-Pentecostal Tradition*).

Some additional firsthand information is available in Denise S. Blakebrough's massive *La Renovación en el Espíritu Santo* (2006), most of which can be found online through Google Books. Blakebrough studied at Duquesne in the 1990s, interviewed Joseph Healy (the chaplain on the Duquesne Weekend), and corresponded with Patrick Bourgeois, whose letters (published by Blakebrough in Spanish) may be the only written source of information on the later lives of Keifer and Storey.

The Duquesne archives contain a 1975 issue of a Catholic newsletter called *A.D.* in which Storey sharply criticized developments within the charismatic renewal.

Alan Schreck, a theology professor at Franciscan University of Steubenville, has provided recent appreciative reflections on the movement in *A Mighty Current of Grace: The Story of the Catholic Charismatic Renewal* (2017).

CHAPTER 5

Interviewees: Reid Carpenter, John Guest, David Hillis, Larry Lloyd, Ruth Malos, Chris Martin, Bill Milliken, Karen Plavan, Terry Webb, David Zubik, Sue Zuk. E-mail correspondence from Mary Beth Gasior and Scott Hahn.

Historical information on the Pittsburgh Leadership Foundation and on Carpenter personally is sadly lacking. Michael Sider-Rose, *Taking the Gospel to the*

NOTE ON SOURCES

Point (2000) is very competent history but ends with the PLF's founding in 1978. David Hillis, *Cities: Playgrounds or Battlegrounds?* (2014), a description of the leadership foundations movement, begins with useful information on Carpenter and the PLF, mostly provided by Carpenter's successor, John Stahl-Wert. Brian Miller of the Center on Faith in Communities wrote a detailed case study (undated, but apparently completed in 2003) on the PLF's operations, with much more extensive description of PLF projects than our chapter offers; see www.centeronfic.org/articles/Pittsburgh.pdf.

Hart Hillman as "the last of the city's great industrial tycoons": This quotation comes from the *Pittsburgh Post-Gazette*'s April 15, 2017 obituary article on Henry Hillman, son of Hart Hillman by his first wife; see www.post-gazette.com/local/city/2017/04/14/Philanthropist-Henry-Hillman-dies/stories/201704140181.

An excellent short history of the Ligonier Valley Study Center is at www.ligonier.org/blog/ligonier-valley-study-center-early-years/.

The Coalition for Christian Outreach, mentioned in the text as a highly successful campus ministry that was born from Pittsburgh Offensive discussions, would have merited its own chapter in this book, but Bob Long had already shared his recollections in great detail for Gary Scott Smith's *A History of Christianity in Pittsburgh* (2018) and was not inclined to do it a second time. Accordingly, we refer you to Smith's book, which has an excellent section on the Coalition's history and impact.

For a brief history of the COAD/CLEAR organization, see www.clearrecovery.org/about-us/clear-history.

"Carole Carpenter Starts New Phase in Her Life," *Ave Herald*, May 31, 2012, www.aveherald.com/news/ave-maria-news/1110-carole-carpenter-starts-new-phase-in-her-life.html, described her work for Ave Maria University.

CHAPTER 6

Interviewees: Michael Baileys, Al Erisman, Paul Limbach, Nancy Alderson McDonnell, Paul McNulty, Sharell Mikesell, Ray Meier, Clair Murphy, Stan Ott, Wayne Thompson, John Turyan.

Nancy Alderson McDonnell generously granted access to the Value of the Person archives, which include Pittron newsletters, countless newspaper articles, and a dozen drafts of a movie script on Alderson's life that never materialized. The archives are heavily weighted toward the 1970s and early 1980s, because after Pittron and several high-profile mediation roles, Alderson's media coverage became largely limited to Labor-Management Prayer Breakfasts, his consideration for Secretary of Labor, and the brief period when he colorfully floated a possible presidential candidacy. McDonnell provided copies of two other primary sources: Alderson's memorial service (including Scott Stevens's message) and Robin Miller's film, *Miracle of Pittron*. She also permitted examination of her organization's files on many of the companies with which Alderson worked most extensively.

R. C. Sproul, *Stronger Than Steel* (1980), is a superb biography, full of insights into Alderson's personal nature and his approach to labor-management relations. In 2014, McDonnell published a new version with an additional chapter that primarily contains Alderson's relation (told in 1989) of his last four days of combat in World War II, along with some reflections by McDonnell on her father's life and its lasting significance.

Wayne T. Alderson and Nancy Alderson McDonnell, *Theory R Management* (1994), is a thorough and rigorous presentation of the Value of the Person approach to managing a workplace. Every organization manager or executive should read it.

The comment about Alderson becoming an elder and later a Christian is two minutes into Al Erisman's tribute to Alderson at a 2014 Faith at Work summit in Boston; the video is at www.youtube.com/watch?v=C7MmUyQ4BwA. Erisman also conducted a detailed interview of Alderson in 2009 for his own magazine, *Ethix*; it can be found at https://ethix.org/2009/10/01/valuing-people-helps-business.

"I knew they were testing me": This comment by Alderson appears in a 1978 article in the Value of the Person archives, covering his speaking appearance in Edmonton, Alberta.

"I made a friend that day and lost my job": John Moody, "Exec Who Championed Bible Class at Glassport Foundry Out of Job," *Pittsburgh Post-Gazette*, February 10, 1975.

"I was this close to saying yes": Erisman 2009 interview.

CHAPTER 7

Interviewees: Geno DeMarco, Hollis Haff, Tunch Ilkin, Jon Kolb, Donnie Shell, Ted Petersen, J. T. Thomas, Calvin Troup, Leo Wisniewski.

Tony Dungy talks about his relationship with Donnie Shell in *Quiet Strength: The Principles, Practices and Priorities of a Winning Life* (2007), 50–57, but we have quoted Shell's recollection of what he said to Dungy at training camp rather than the slightly different version in Dungy's book.

The Philadelphia Eagles' faith-based video (2017) is available at www.youtube.com/watch?v=6bnEY13vAok.

Gary Scott Smith, *A History of Christianity in Pittsburgh* (2018), has a chronologically more expansive chapter on Christian members of the Steelers from the 1970s to the 2010s, including detailed sections on Terry Bradshaw, Ben Roethlisberger, and Troy Polamalu.

Gary Pomerantz, *Their Life's Work: The Brotherhood of the 1970s Pittsburgh Steelers, Then and Now* (2013), is a revealing, extensively researched, entertaining work but says barely a word about any of the players' spiritual lives.

CHAPTER 8

Interviewees: Rosie Fyfe, Austin Gohn, Mary Hays, Whis Hays, Rich Herbster, John Macdonald, Steve Noll, Robert Osborne, John Rodgers, Joel Scandrett, Laurie Thompson. E-mail correspondence from Robert Duncan.

NOTE ON SOURCES

Janet Leighton, *Lift High the Cross*, updated and expanded edition (2014), is an excellent, detailed history of Trinity School for Ministry.

D. A. Carson described his visit to Alf Stanway in *A Call to Spiritual Reformation: Priorities from Paul and His Prayers* (1992).

The quotation from Jeremy Bonner, *Called Out of Darkness: A History of the Episcopal Diocese of Pittsburgh, 1750–2006* (2009), appears on 267–68.

Stephen Noll, *The Global Anglican Communion: Contending for Anglicanism, 1993–2018* (2018), contains an annotated collection of his essays in the Episcopal/Anglican battles.

Miranda Hassett, *Anglican Communion in Crisis: How Episcopal Dissidents and Their African Allies Are Reshaping Anglicanism* (2007), offers some observations on the role of Trinity and its staff (primarily Rodgers and Noll) in the alliance between conservative Anglicans in the United States and Africa.

CHAPTER 9

Interviewees: Marion Adams, Russell Boston, Floyd Cephas, William Glaze, Joanne Anderson Purcell, Dolores Speaks, Chuck and Bobi Tame. E-mail correspondence from Richard Allen Farmer.

Bethany has extensive archives including a history of the congregation. The archives contain news articles on the church's interaction with the DMX, as well as the correspondence between the DMX and Pastor Farmer.

A brief discussion of efforts to desegregate Pittsburgh's swimming pools and roller rinks in the 1950s appears in Joe W. Trotter and Jared N. Day, *Race and Renaissance: African Americans in Pittsburgh since World War II* (2010), 87–89. See also Linda Wilson Fuoco, "Local Activists, Black and White, Worked To Integrate Sully's Pool in South Park," *Pittsburgh Post-Gazette*, February 21, 2001, http://old.post-gazette.com/neigh_south/20010221spool2.asp.

CHAPTER 10

Interviewees: Kathy and Bruce Bain, Bryan McCabe, Susie McCabe, John Nuzzo, Jay Passavant, Arlene Rink, Jan Sherman, Grant Smith, Chris White, Blaine Workman. Additional background conversations with North Way staff. E-mail correspondence from Lisa Anderson.

Gary Scott Smith's *A History of Christianity in Pittsburgh* (2018) highlights North Way as one of its four featured megachurches, briefly discussing its history but focusing primarily on the church's status and activities at the time of writing.

Article on North Way's planned expansion (which never happened): Karen Kane and Ervin Dyer, "Two Huge Churches Follow the Signs into North Hills," *Pittsburgh Post-Gazette*, February 8, 2002, http://old.post-gazette.com/neigh_north/20020208churchboom0208p2.asp.

The discussion of the succession process draws heavily from Jay Passavant, *Seamless Succession* (2015).

CHAPTER 11

Report on the 2009–2016 dialogue between the World Evangelical Alliance and the Vatican: http://www.vatican.va/roman_curia/pontifical_councils/chrstuni/evangelicals-docs/rc_pc_chrstuni_doc_20171017_comm-report-2009-2016_en.html.

Antwaan Randle El's appearance at the Bible Chapel: Jan Ackerman, "The Steelers; Antwaan Randle El Tells Peters Congregation Bible Is the Game Plan of Life," *Pittsburgh Post-Gazette*, February 13, 2006, www.post-gazette.com/sports/steelers/2006/02/13/The-Steelers-Antwaan-Randle-El-tells-Peters-congregation-Bible-is-the-game-plan-of-life/stories/200602130084.